Pen in Hand: Children Become Writers

Bernice E. Cullinan
Editor

International Reading Association
Newark, Delaware 19714, USA

The International Reading Association attempts, through its publications, to provide a forum for a wide spectrum of opinions on reading. This policy permits divergent viewpoints without assuming the endorsement of the Association.

Director of Publications Joan M. Irwin
Managing Editor Anne Fullerton
Associate Editor Romayne McElhaney
Assistant Editor Amy Trefsger
Editorial Assistant Janet Parrack
Production Department Manager Iona Sauscermen
Graphic Design Coordinator Boni Nash
Design Consultant Larry Husfelt
Desktop Publishing Supervisor Wendy Mazur
Desktop Publishing Anette Schuetz-Ruff
                        Cheryl Strum
                        Richard James
Proofing Florence Pratt

"Call the Periods Call the Commas" on page 60 is from Kalli Dakos's *If You're Not Here, Please Raise Your Hand: Poems about School*, copyright ©1990, published by Four Winds Press, an imprint of Macmillan Publishing Co. Reprinted by permission of the publisher. Illustrations are by Dave Bailey.

Every effort has been made to trace and acknowledge copyright holders of material from other sources included in this work. The publisher welcomes any information that will lead to correction or clarification of such acknowledgments in future printings.

Library of Congress Cataloging in Publication Data
Pen in hand: children become writers/Bernice E. Cullinan, editor.
    p. cm.
Includes bibliographical references and indexes.
1. Language Arts—United States. 2. English language—Composition and exercises—Study and teaching—United States. 3. Children—United States—Books and reading.
I. Cullinan, Bernice E.
LB1576.P367 1993   93-25880
372.6—dc20 CIP
ISBN 0-87207-383-1

Contents

Foreword

Children become writers because their teachers write...and read, listen, and then share their literate world with them. I am struck by the literacy of the authors in this book. They know and experience the world of children's literature. Their literate eyes spot the teachable moment in both the young author's written text and in the book that young author is reading.

This book offers sound methods that will help children become better writers. From it you will learn how to bring writing and reading more closely together and will note good commonsense teaching methods. Such perplexing areas as helping to bring out the voice of the child in his or her nonfiction writing and teaching conventions within a framework of children's literature are covered here. *Pen in Hand*, however, offers something of far greater significance than methodologies. The authors in this text understand the *conditions* of literacy in the classroom that help children become lifelong writers, readers, and thinkers. Take this book seriously and *your* children will become those lifelong writers.

I still remember the smell in Miss Fitch's classroom. The odors were curious, dank and moldy. Today, at 63 years of age, the smell of a mushroom still takes me back to that room 47 years ago and all the artifacts it contained. I see the stuffed snowy owl, shark's jaws, jars with cocoons, bird charts, snakes, and tanks of creatures in formaldehyde. Yesterday I ran across bear and moose scat in the woods next to my home and I heard Miss Fitch's voice: "What do you make of this?" Her question carried a tone of wonder and the taste of expectation. Her question didn't know its own answer. Rather, the question was one of invitation to a world she knew well yet still wanted to discover with me.

I remember none of Miss Fitch's methods but I remember her way of looking at the world and the questions that naturally arose when she addressed it. Sitting in her classroom I had the feeling that something wonderful might be just around the bend of the next dilemma. Best of all, she sensed that something remarkable might come from our mouths, something she'd never heard before. She might have known of Robert Frost's simple statement at the beginning of his classes: "Surprise me." I am struck by how easily and willingly the authors in this book are surprised by what children write, read, and learn.

Neil Simon, Broadway playwright, struggled with the anatomy of writing comedy through a description of two characters in *Broadway Bound*:

> Stan keeps asking Eugene for the essential ingredient in comedy, and when Eugene can't answer, Stan says, "Conflict!" When he asks for the other key ingredient and Eugene can only come up with "More conflict?" Stan says, "The key word is wants. In every comedy, even drama, somebody has to want something and want it bad. When somebody tries to stop him—that's conflict" (1992).

I've learned from the authors in this book and a host of teachers like Nancie Atwell, Linda Rief, and Mary Ellen Giacobbe that an essential condition in the literate classroom is sensing the "want" in the child, the interest, the "chutzpah" mentioned by Shelley Harwayne in the second chapter. Somehow Miss Fitch found out about my interest in birds and hybridizing gladioluses and through those interests brought me into her specialty, biology.

Of course, *we* are the chief condition in the classroom. It is the quality of questions we ask *ourselves* when we write and read that establishes the conditions that invite children to be lifelong readers and writers. Vera John-Steiner in *Notebooks of the Mind* (1985) shows us with the people she interviewed in her study how important it is for children to observe the way adults think and learn. Children "hang around" our literate lives. They literally breathe the atmospheres set by our struggles to write with them and by the questions we ask ourselves when we read the books they read.

Children observe us. Why not take advantage of this powerful opportunity for teaching? Do you doubt that children observe you? Park your new used car in the parking lot at school and within minutes the children will be discussing the efficacy of your choice. Wear new earrings or a necktie, walk in with a new briefcase, put on new perfume or aftershave; they observe and discuss.

In 1978 I conducted a study for the Ford Foundation on the status of writing in the United States. Part of the investigation included interviewing people from all walks of life to gain some sense of their educational history and then to place writing within the context of their education. Toward the end of the interview we asked, "Tell us about a teacher who saw something in you worth writing about and then helped you write it." Sixty-five percent of the respondents had *no* teacher who ever helped them write. Approximately 30 percent had *one* teacher. Another 5 percent had *two* teachers. No one had more than two. If, however, respondents had had one teacher who helped them write, they could describe that teacher in detail. Further, the one teacher had made a significant difference if their lives.

Read and enjoy this book. Invite children into your world of writing and reading as the authors of this book have done. Be that one teacher who observes what children have to say and shows them how to write it.

Donald H. Graves
University of New Hampshire

References

Graves, D.H. (1978). *Balance the basics: Let them write*. New York: Ford Foundation.

John-Steiner, V. (1985). *Notebooks of the mind*. Albuquerque, NM: University of New Mexico Press.

Simon, N. (1992, Winter). The art of the theatre x. *Paris Review, 125*.

Contributors

Bernice E. Cullinan
New York University
New York, New York

Roger Farr
Indiana University
Bloomington, Indiana

Ralph Fletcher
Durham, New Hampshire

Shelley Harwayne
Manhattan New School
New York, New York

Ann K. Lovett
Munsey Park School
Manhasset, New York

Elisabeth Meltzer
Sea Cliff School
Sea Cliff, New York

JoAnne Sangirardi-Gray
Sea Cliff School
Sea Cliff, New York

Virginia C. Schroder
Munsey Park School
Manhasset, New York

Introduction

Bernice E. Cullinan

Children are the messages we send into a future we will not see. Teachers know that eventually we must send children out into the world to stand alone, to become independent learners, to express themselves clearly, to make worthwhile contributions to society, and to create a humane life for themselves and those around them. We guide them as readers, writers, speakers, and thinkers, but we cannot go with them—nor do we know the world they will inherit.

During the past year, the International Reading Association published *Children's Voices*, a book on talk in the classroom, and *Fact and Fiction*, one on literature across the curriculum; this book, a companion to those two volumes, is about children's writing. At first glance, these works may not seem to be within the province of reading. They are, however, integral to reading and are topics necessary for successful teaching of reading.

Using literature across the curriculum helps students learn language, learn through language, and learn about language. These areas interconnect; they form part of an interwoven pattern that

1

includes reading, writing, listening, and speaking—the language arts. Reading teachers know that we need to engage students in writing if we want to teach them how to read. We know that teaching students reading without including writing is like teaching them to swim with one hand tied behind them. We realize that talking and listening are important ways to learn.

Below are some understandings teachers have about writing, reading, talking, listening, and thinking:

Writing and reading are closely related. Writing and reading are two sides of the same coin. Both processes involve creating meaning through print.

Writing creates the need to read, just as reading can create the need to write. When we write we discover areas in which we need more information. If we need new ways to solve a writing problem, face a dilemma in writing, need inspiration to write more and to write better, we stop writing and start reading. By the same token, we often feel a need to write or talk after reading. When we are filled with emotion from reading we want to express it by writing or talking about what we feel.

Writers become better readers. Readers become better writers. No writer ever became a writer without reading. In *The Writing Life*, Annie Dillard (1989) describes how writers study literature—not necessarily the world itself. If they buy a hamburger or take an airplane ride, it may have no effect on their writing and they will probably spare their readers a report of the experience. But writers are careful about what they read, for that *will* become part of what they write. What we read shapes what we write. No matter what we start out to write, we end up being affected by what we read.

Writing and talking are interrelated. Writing and talking are both expressive skills. We must formulate what we want to say in speech or in writing. In the creative act of putting words together to express thoughts, children draw on the same linguistic storehouse of possibilities whether they are reading, writing, talking, or thinking.

Writing improves talking. Talking improves writing. Children shape meaning at the point of utterance—or at the point of a pencil. They find out what they want to say by expressing it. An idea developed in *Children's Voices* is that we find out what we think by seeing what we say, that expressing an idea helps clarify it. E.M. Forster reported hearing someone say, "How do I know what I think until I see what I say?" This thought-clarification process applies to speech as well as to writing. We call it "finding your voice."

Children use the same underlying processes to construct meaning from print that they use to develop meaning from oral language. They first make gross approximations—unskilled attempts to construct meaning—and then move from broad general strokes to more specific discriminations. Beginning writers and readers use pictures and other nonlinguistic cues to identify the books they want to hear over and over again. Young writers start writing by drawing pictures to find out what they want to say. Gradually they learn to make distinctions among letter forms and word meanings.

Ralph Fletcher begins *Pen in Hand*'s discussion of writing by demonstrating how children's literature gives young writers their wings; he also points out that children need to have firm roots in actual experience to make their writing real and meaningful. In addition to his metaphor of roots and wings, Ralph creates vivid images about writing and fundamental human processes: cooking, living, and building. He discusses three levels of involvement: marinating children in literature, allowing them to dwell in literature, and building on experiences with literature. Each of these levels adds to the texture and substance of writing.

Shelley Harwayne shows the chutzpah young writers display in choosing titles when they write nonfiction reports. Their titles promise "All You Ever Wanted to Know about Gerbils" or "The World's Greatest Report on Guinea Pigs," but the body or substance of their reports sometimes falls short. Shelley discusses three major lessons she learned from observing professional writers at work; she draws implications for classrooms from them. This chapter shows how we can help students live up to the promise of their titles by helping them learn strategies adult writers use, such as how to collect information in research, to organize it, and to synthesize it.

Virginia Schroder and Ann Lovett heard about writing process workshops and thought they would like to try this approach, but they couldn't find anyone to help them translate theory into practice in their early elementary classrooms. They understood the concepts intellectually and wanted support to establish procedures that would work with their students. They describe their search for information and guidance and show how they took their first tentative steps to risk sharing their own writing to model the process for their students.

JoAnne Sangirardi-Gray and Elisabeth Meltzer responded to pressure from their colleagues to include mechanics in their writing workshops. They did not "teach the basics" in a traditional way, however. Instead they developed their own philosophy and created a different approach to reach their objectives. These two author-teachers contend that it is necessary to create the need to learn a skill before it is taught. When young writers learn a skill in the context of using it, the skill makes sense to them; they remember it, know when to use it, and recognize the reason for it. JoAnne and Elisabeth believe that the content of writing is most important—mechanics only help to clarify it. In their classrooms they maintain the conditions they know young writers need in order to write, while helping them develop skill with mechanics "organically" in the process of writing.

Roger Farr brings the sharp objective eye of the researcher to the use of writing in response to reading as a tool for assessment. He makes it clear that if we want to pursue portfolio assessment and whole language programs and allow students the freedom to choose what they read and write about, we must remember that we need to be accountable to parents, school boards, administrators, and ultimately society. We need to find ways to demonstrate that our students are reading and writing more, reading and writing better, and loving what they are doing. That is a challenge we face together.

The purpose of IRA's series on reading, writing, talking, and using literature across the curriculum is to provide busy teachers with practical help. Teachers are too pressed for time to read all the research and translate it into practice; they often find it difficult to learn about what other teachers do and to share their own success stories. This book and its companions, written by people who work with children every day, are intended to give teachers ideas that will work for them—and for the children we are sending into a future we will not see.

Reference

Dillard, A. (1989). *The writing life*. New York: HarperCollins.

Chapter 1

Roots and Wings: Literature and Children's Writing

Ralph Fletcher

When I finished reading *The Two of Them* by Aliki, the second graders remained silent. You could actually see a residue of sorrow on their faces. This picture book about the love between a grandfather and granddaughter and her sadness at his death would echo inside them for a long time.

A curly-haired boy broke the silence with a squeaky voice. "My grandpa died, too," he said.

Now other children began sharing their reactions to this book, although one girl was noticeably silent. When the time came to write, she ran back to her seat and swiftly got to work. The other children began writing on a variety of topics—birthdays, skiing, an argument with an evil little sister—but Christine chose to borrow the theme from Aliki's book. Here's what she wrote:

> Just like in the story the two of them my grandpa gave
> Heather my sister a necklise and when I was born my grandpa
> gave me a ring and last year it fit and this year he died. He
> died January 5, 1991, the beginning of the year. When I went
> to his house we played cards and we also played a guessing
> game. And we planted flowers. And when he died my grand-
> ma tolled me that the flowers died. I was the one who cryed
> the most. My Mom's friend Ilean took us for some pizza, and
> to see Home Alone, and then to friendlys. He didn't want a
> funeral so that night we went to see him before he went away.
> I bought him some flowers and I used all my money and I'm
> still broke. And when I was born he said: "Thank god its
> another girl the army can't take her away" (Fletcher, 1993).

It has been said that the two most precious gifts an adult
can give a child are roots and wings: a solid foundation coupled
with the courage and confidence to pursue big dreams. Books can
give children parallel gifts. Through books students take root in our
literary tradition; books help children begin to internalize myriad
conventions of language. Books teach skills and techniques ranging
from the most concrete (punctuation, paragraphing) to the most
ephemeral (metaphor, rhythm, tension, foreshadowing). Children
draw on what they know about books when they begin to write
coherent narratives.

Books were my mentors when I started writing. Anything
by E.B. White. *Housekeeping* by Marilynne Robinson. *One Flew
over the Cuckoo's Nest* by Ken Kesey. Jack London's story "To
Build a Fire" made me want to make other people feel the same
savage intensity about life that London had made me feel. Reading
made me want to write.

Our classrooms can be literate environments in which
poems and stories spark our students' imaginations and open possibilities they never dreamed of for their own writing. We can
encourage young writers to take inspiration from books they know
by following a three-tiered approach:

- Marinate students in the best literature we can find.
- Find authentic ways to invite students to dwell in those books, stories, and poems, so they come to know these works from the inside out.
- Once students have a common experience in certain books, begin to explore with them the composing techniques used by the professional writers who wrote those books.

Marinating

It's no secret that reading and writing have many links. Both activities immerse us in a process of actively using language to make meaning of the world; both involve a great deal of revision; the reader and the writer both conduct a "dialogue with an emerging text" (Calkins, 1983).

We need to marinate students in literature so that, over time, it soaks into their consciousness and, eventually, into their writing. JoAnn Curtis recently said to me, "We need to create classrooms that are giant invitations to read." We can do this by filling our classroom libraries with books—lots of them. We also need to provide students with frequent opportunities to immerse themselves in those books, beginning on the first day of school in the earliest grades. Some first grade teachers set the stage for reading and let parents know that books will be important in their classrooms by sending notes to the homes of incoming students before the school year begins. These notes can deliver the message by saying something as simple as "Please send your child to school with his or her favorite book. We'll be sharing our favorites in class during the first week of school."

Reading aloud, of course, is the single most powerful way of bringing literature to students. Children should be read to every day. No one would quibble with these statements if I were talking exclusively about primary children, and I think it's true that most kindergarten, first, and second grade teachers regularly read aloud to their students. But fewer teachers read aloud to students in fourth, fifth, and sixth grade, and fewer still read aloud to students in grades seven and eight. This may be a serious mistake. Trelease (1990) points out that most children are better able to process information aurally than visually. In fact, the average student's capacity for processing print typically does not equal capacity for processing spoken language until around grade eight. If we don't read aloud to older children, we deny them the enhanced comprehension that comes from listening to books. And we deny them the pleasure of hearing books read beautifully by a skilled reader.

A few common-sense thoughts about reading aloud to young writers:

Read books you love. In his *New York Times* review of Jane Yolen's *Owl Moon,* novelist Paul Johnson wrote, "The very best books for not-quite-reading children must be written to charm and astonish the adults who will read them aloud: thrill that reader, who will communicate the prickles at the nape of the neck, and you'll have created a desire in the young listener to learn how to read books alone" (1988).

Children will be alive not just to the book you read but to the relationship between you and the book. I vividly recall watching editor and writer Adrian Peetoom give a passionate reading of Mary Ann Hoberman's *A House Is a House for Me.* I still can't pick up that book without thinking of his reading of it, a reading that was my first experience of the story.

Parents and administrators may react with arched eyebrows at the idea of fifth or sixth grade teachers reading picture books to their students. But picture books have many advantages for the reading-writing classroom. They are short and digestible—meant to be read in a single sitting—and give the reader the satisfaction of hearing the entire story at one time. The best books of this genre are beautifully written and contain many familiar literary elements—protagonist, setting, conflict, tension, climax, resolution, and so forth—that teachers point out in novel units. When I do encounter older children who smirk at picture books, I make a point of reading aloud a few powerful examples of this genre: *Nettie's Trip South* by Ann Turner, *Faithful Elephants* by Yukio Tsuchiya, *A Father Like That* by Charlotte Zolotow. Potent picture books like these will usually put any skepticism to rest.

Develop a chemistry with the books you read aloud. This is time well spent. Practice reading aloud to your partner, daughter, grandson, cat. Once you become comfortable with a book and know it well, you can relax, fill your rendition with meaning and emotion, and make eye contact with students while reading aloud.

Beware of interrupting or dissecting the reading. A book, like a joke, has a cadence, a rhythm. A good reader always stays with the book's rhythm. You risk destroying that rhythm if you stop frequently to summarize, teach vocabulary, or lead students through laborious exercises in prediction. I believe every child has a right to hear a first reading of a book or a poem in a straightforward, uninterrupted fashion. You can always go back and point out specifics or teach lessons in a rereading.

Make time for response. Every student will have some reaction to the book you read. If, however, you launch immediately into a classroom discussion, only the most assertive students will get the chance to verbalize their reactions. Other, more timid students will be left with responses that are unarticulated and partially formed. Children need to talk about books to find out what they have to say.

Come up with a structure that allows each student to respond individually before a class discussion. (Otherwise students will tend toward "group think.") A student's first response to a piece of literature should be allowed to be as open-ended and unguided as possible. You might ask students to turn to a friend and talk for two or three minutes. Petrosky (1988) suggests that students internalize concepts of literature more readily through authentic, student-to-student "cross-talk" than through traditional teacher-student dialogue. With older students, talk could be alternated with a few minutes of writing in reading logs or response journals.

Dwelling

"The best way to improve a student's writing is to wake up the reader within that student," JoAnn Curtis once said to me. "Once the reader is awake and listening, we can speak to the reader in the child during a writing conference."

For many children, the internal reader wakes slowly and fitfully. We can help rouse our young readers by creating a classroom atmosphere that invites children to climb inside books, spend time there, and savor what they find so they come to know books from the inside out. The trick, of course, is not to give students literature-based busywork but rather to provide meaningful reasons for students to stay with the books they encounter.

A few suggestions:

Rereading. "I read everything twice," novelist Robert Cohen (1988) says. "Once to enjoy it, and a second time to steal everything from the author. By that I mean I'm trying to learn how the author put the book together." In a first reading, the reader focuses on what happens in the story. When the reader rereads, the focus shifts and the reader may begin to wonder about the writing itself. How did the author do this? What are the techniques that created this effect? In the long run, such wondering nourishes the young writer far more than the ability to recapitulate what the book is about.

A writer's notebook. Many writers keep a notebook in which they jot down passages from the books they read. The notebook becomes a vessel that holds striking beginnings or stirring endings, memorable descriptions, evocative sentences, or unusual words that affected the writer in some way when she or he encountered them. Students can keep such notebooks and peruse them occasionally to find inspiration for their own writing. Invite students to set up sections in their notebooks—"Leads," "Setting," "Unforgettable Language," "Endings," "Characterization"—or to create sections of their own choosing. This will help them organize the passages they wish to record and set up a way of locating particular entries when the notebooks are referred to later. (For more ideas on the writer's notebook, see Calkins, 1990.)

Student read-aloud. Encourage students to practice reading aloud to one another. If it's true that knowing something well means being able to teach it to someone else, then one way of knowing a book well means being able to read it aloud confidently to another person. Have students practice reading their favorite picture books or poems out loud. Encourage them to practice until they can read with inflection and look up occasionally from the page. Children can enjoy these read-alouds in small groups of peers; alternatively, upper grade children might be paired with primary or preschool children to provide the older students with practice in reading aloud while giving the younger students extra exposure to books.

Choral reading. Predictable books or books with repeated phrases lend themselves to choral readings. In a choral reading, a group of students (four to six is ideal) look carefully at a book or poem to decide how to read it aloud. What are the most important parts? Who will read which parts? Which parts should be read by the whole group? Should the voices get softer or sadder at certain parts? Should there be any movement or action during the reading?

Author Bill Martin Jr (1991) once remarked that children need to take book language and transform it in some way to make it their own. Choral reading encourages students to explore a text deeply through readings and rereadings that take place while students practice. This allows students to internalize the text and gradually put their own "spin" on the language. Choral readings are particularly helpful for hesitant, word-by-word readers because they allow such students to get swept up in the rhythm and melody of the language.

Drawing. Heard (1989) suggests that students of all ages make drawings in response to poems. Drawing helps students internalize poetry by visualizing the images at its heart.

Author studies. Author studies provide another means of inviting students to delve deeply into books, in this case those by a particular author. Author studies, like choral readings, can be undertaken in student groups. I once observed a group of third graders study 20 picture books by Byrd Baylor over a few days. They then made an oral presentation to the class. "She almost always writes about the desert," Lisa explained. "And she likes to write about things that are very old—like rocks, fossils, or just things that happened a long time ago."

"Her books are like poetry," Paul put in. "When you read the book it's like you're reading poems. Listen to this."

These students had moved well beyond the typical, dreary "This book is about..." book report. They spoke with the confidence of insiders. This is precisely the goal of routines and activities that encourage children to dwell in books.

Teaching from Common Ground

Students who know even five or ten books inside out have a genuine chance of understanding and appreciating many complex strategies available to them when they write. I will consider strategies involved with solving two common writing difficulties here, but there are certainly many more strategies to be learned from literature.

Details: The art of specificity. Anyone who has taught writing has exhorted students with words like these: "Put details into your writing! Specific details give readers a picture of what is happening!" Certainly true, and there is no shortage of children's literature to demonstrate this point. But the art of specificity goes beyond the mere inclusion of details. Here's a secret that writers know: specific details mentioned early in a story usually return, often with more significance, toward the end. Anton Chekhov once wrote, "If in the first chapter you say that a gun hung on the wall, in the second or third chapter it must without fail be discharged" (quoted in Murray, 1990). No accident that Brian receives a hatchet early in Gary Paulsen's *Hatchet*—that tool will help him survive later on. Such a detail is crucial to setting up the events that follow.

In Aliki's *The Two of Them*, the grandfather makes a ring for his granddaughter on the day of her birth. The girl grows up, sharing adventures and quiet times with him. The ring is not mentioned again until the end of the book. The girl has grown up, the ring now fits, but the grandfather has begun to fail. In this story, the ring works on many levels: a keepsake, a sign of the girl's coming of age, and a symbol suggesting the circularity of life.

Young writers also frequently have difficulty deciding which details are important. The much maligned bed-to-bed story results from a student's inability to exclude any event—no matter how insignificant or unimportant—from a particular day. This equal attention to all details weakens a story by creating a "shopping list" effect that forces the reader to do the hard work of sifting the wheat from the chaff. By following the examples of skilled writers, children can learn how to emphasize some details and events, cut others, and slow down at the crucial moment so the reader can fully absorb the drama taking place.

Time. Inexperienced writers are typically controlled by the element of time in their stories. Through frequent encounters with literature, young writers can discover techniques for controlling the time in their stories so time won't control them. One way of accomplishing this is by learning how to focus on one small slice of a day. Maxine Kumin's lovely picture book *The Beach before Breakfast* provides a fine example of this technique.

In many books, page one leads to page two which leads to page three—and so on through a chronological sequence. But other books are a collection of snapshots loosely held together and not linked in a linear progression. These books often provide sketches of particular characters. *Rosalie* by Joan Hewett, a portrait of a much-loved family dog, is among my favorites of this genre.

Flashback, when used with the appropriate transitional words, can be a powerful alternative to the straight chronological narrative. Many books use flashback: *A Chair for My Mother* by Vera Williams, *Wilfrid Gordon McDonald Partridge* by Mem Fox, and *Tar Beach* by Faith Ringgold, to name just three of the best. Patricia MacLachlan's *Sarah, Plain and Tall* begins with a flashback to the mother's death. And in *Julie of the Wolves* by Jean Craighead George, the entire middle section consists of flashbacks to events in Julie's unhappy marriage. Books like these give students potential tools for playing with time in their own writing.

Students also need help in slowing time at the crucial moment of a story so the reader can fully absorb the drama taking place. Slowing the action with a dramatic scene is a device many writers use to great effect: for example, consider Barbara Shook Hazen's *Tight Times* and Cynthia Rylant's *Miss Maggie.*

Scarlett, a fifth grader, wrote a story about her family. Her first draft quickly summarized her family's first encounter with her adopted brother. In a second draft, she crafted this dramatic scene that allows the reader to relish the moment:

I had been waiting for this moment for almost two years. My adopted brother was going to be arriving from Korea in only a moment. Suddenly a lady came off the plane. She told us the boy was very excited but also very shy. Then she walked back a little into the walkway from the plane. When she came back to us she was holding a Korean/Black boy's hand. He was simply adorable.

He had jet black hair and his skin was the color of chocolate milk. He bowed his head shyly and never spoke unless the lady asked him a question. Even then he gave short answers and spoke in a low tone. I sat in a chair and gazed at him while my mother and father talked with the woman with huge grins on their faces.

"This is Lee Yong Seok," she said.

My mom got on her knees and took his hand. She could hardly speak. All she said was "Hi." My dad stepped right up and tickled him. Yong Seok didn't seem to mind. He started laughing, playing. My dad was really excited. He hung the laughing boy upside down and tickled him some more. Soon Yong Seok was on the red carpeted floor of the airport laughing as hard as he could. Mom and I thought he would burst from laughing so hard. My dad kept repeating: "My little boy, my little boy," so many times I couldn't count them.

Opening the Door

The connections children make between the books they read and their own writing do not happen in an instant by means of a worksheet, a carefully orchestrated class project, or even frequent read-aloud sessions. The reading-writing connection is an important spark that happens within each student. Internal connections take time. The process can be slow and painstaking; moreover, this process cannot be forced. It's important to remember what Holdaway (1979) says about real learning: it is always self-initiated, self-monitored, and self-paced.

The students in our classrooms will tell us when they are ready to take the techniques gleaned from literature and bring them into their own writing. Books open the door; each young writer decides when to enter. If we watch, if we are patient, we can bring books to our young writers in a way that will give them the roots and wings they need for the journey ahead.

References

Calkins, L.M. (1983). *Lessons from a child.* Portsmouth, NH: Heinemann.

Calkins, L.M. (1990). *Living between the lines.* Portsmouth, NH: Heinemann.

Cohen, R. (1988, July). Paper presented at Teachers College, Columbia University, New York, NY.

Fletcher, R. (1993). *What a writer needs.* Portsmouth, NH: Heinemann.

Heard, G. (1989). *For the good of the earth and the sun.* Portsmouth, NH: Heinemann.

Holdaway, D. (1979). *The foundations of literacy.* New York: Scholastic.

Johnson, P. (1988, January 3). Review of Jane Yolen's *Owl Moon. New York Times Book Review.*

Martin, B., Jr. (1991). [Interview conducted by R. Fletcher.] In N. Atwell (Ed.), *Workshop 3: The politics of process.* Portsmouth, NH: Heinemann.

Murray, D.M. (1990). *Shoptalk.* Portsmouth, NH: Boynton/Cook.

Petrosky, A. (1988, July). Workshop conducted at Teachers College, Columbia University, New York, NY.

Trelease, J. (1990, September). Speech delivered at Paramus High School, Paramus, NJ.

Literature

Aliki. (1979). *The two of them.* New York: Greenwillow.

Fox, M. (1985). *Wilfrid Gordon McDonald Partridge.* Brooklyn, NY: Kane/Miller.

George, J.C. (1972). *Julie of the wolves.* New York: Harper Trophy.

Hazen, B.S. (1979). *Tight times.* New York: Viking.

Hewett, J. (1987). *Rosalie.* New York: Lothrop, Lee & Shepard.

Hoberman, M.A. (1978). *A house is a house for me.* New York: Viking.

Kesey, K. (1962). *One flew over the cuckoo's nest.* New York: Viking.

Kumin, M. (1964). *The beach before breakfast.* New York: Putnam.

London, J. (1963). To build a fire. In J. London, *White Fang and other stories.* New York: Dodd, Mead.

MacLachlan, P. (1985). *Sarah, plain and tall.* New York: HarperCollins.

Paulsen, G. (1987). *Hatchet.* New York: Penguin.

Ringgold, F. (1991). *Tar beach.* New York: Crown.

Robinson, M. (1980). *Housekeeping.* New York: Farrar, Straus & Giroux.

Rylant, C. (1983). *Miss Maggie.* New York: Dutton.

Tsuchiya, Y. (1951). *Faithful elephants.* Boston, MA: Houghton Mifflin.

Turner, A. (1987). *Nettie's trip south.* New York: Macmillan.

Williams, V. (1982). *A chair for my mother.* New York: Greenwillow.

Yolen, J. (1987). *Owl moon.* New York: Philomel.

Zolotow, C. (1971). *A father like that.* New York: HarperCollins.

Chapter 2

Chutzpah and the Nonfiction Writer*

Shelley Harwayne

ve Mutchnick, a kindergarten teacher in New York City, approached one of the five-year-olds in her class and asked, "What are you writing?"

"I'm writing about infection."

"Oh, really," Eve responded, highly impressed. "You mean germs and viruses?"

"No, infection. You know—real stuff, true stuff. Like this book about ghosts—that's fection. But this book about different kinds of houses—that's infection." Of course, teachers, writers, librarians, and booksellers know "infection" by the name "nonfiction"—that is,

---

* This chapter has been adapted from a speech delivered to participants at the Teachers College Writing Project Summer Institute in the Teaching of Writing and Reading in July 1989.

informational books or writing about real stuff, true stuff. Perhaps surprisingly, when I think about nonfiction writing, I think of *chutzpah,* the Yiddish word for gall, guts, nerve, or brazenness. Often chutzpah has a negative connotation. For example, if someone cuts you off in city traffic to beat you to a parking space and then asks you for change for the meter, you might say, "What chutzpah he's got!" Susan Ohanian recently used the word in a most clever way. The last line of her critique of E.D. Hirsch's *Cultural Literacy* reads, "'Chutzpah' is on his list, and his book is full of it" (1987, p. 22). But chutzpah can also be used in a positive way. For example, one night my daughter came home and told my husband and me about a boy she had seen on the Staten Island ferry. He was wearing a gold earring in the shape of a swastika. She had approached him, asked if he knew what the symbol represented, and then told him how offensive she found it. Of course, my husband and I lectured her about not talking to—let alone reprimanding—strangers, but when she left the room we talked about what chutzpah she has. She's bold and confident in a positive "go for it," outspoken, lively sort of way. She's not afraid to speak her mind, accept big challenges, and make her voice heard.

When I look through files of student nonfiction writing, I never fail to think about the chutzpah many children have, and it is my daughter's sort of chutzpah that I mean. The titles of these written reports alone indicate how very sure these children are of themselves: "The Great Gerbil Report"; "All You Need to Know about Guinea Pigs"; "A World Full of Information on Gymnastics"; and "The Greatest Report on Earth about Bees, Wasps, and Hornets." It takes a lot of chutzpah to be as bold and presumptuous as these titles suggest, and I believe that by encouraging this sort of chutzpah we will help children to improve not only their writing, but also their images of and confidence in themselves.

But how far does this natural chutzpah go in children's writing? Young authors' boldness—and pride—in their nonfiction writing frequently extends beyond the titles they choose and into the wording of their dedications, prologues, and About the Author pages. To introduce her report on seals, for example, one child wrote as follows:

No, not eels, seals
Not big deals, big seals.
Not fishing reels, big *seals.*
This book is not on *eels,*
big deals,
or fishing reels.
Just seals.

This prologue to a report on penguins is also filled with wonderful chutzpah:

Old Grandma Hubbard went to the Antarctic to get her poor dog a bone when she got there A penguin was there and now my story has begun. Old Grandma Hubbard learned from the penguins all she could learn about penguins, and THIS IS WHAT SHE LEARNED.

There's something very charming about children who are so sure of themselves. Their writing seems full of that hard-to-define quality of voice.

When I read further into children's reports, however, I often find myself growing frustrated. It seems that these young writers put energy only into the frills, the packaging of their work—titles, dedications, prologues, and epilogues. These are usually the only pages I want to show off to my colleagues or make into over-heads for inservice presentations. The reports themselves lack the same spirit and engaging voice. For instance, the penguin report that began with so much enthusiasm goes on in routine fashion to say that "there are 17 species of penguins. Penguins are birds that can't fly. They are black with a white chest." Children do seem to have chutzpah in their writing, but only when it comes to prettying up the product and adding the Madison Avenue touches of colored binders, glossaries, and photographs. I've come to believe that in order to carry their energy through an entire piece of nonfiction writing, children need chutzpah in the process of researching, plan-ning, dreaming, and creating—in the entire process of learning and writing about their topics.

Not long ago, I spent time interviewing people who take their nonfiction writing seriously. I was following Calkins's advice: "We need to study how real researchers go about their work and to use this as the basis for units on report writing" (1989, pp. 272-273). I spoke to teacher-researchers, doctoral students, children's authors, freelance writers, and my colleagues from the Teachers College Writing Project. I learned that all of them are full of chutzpah—in a most positive, admirable sort of way. They are aggressive, bold, assertive, and full of spirit *throughout* the process of composing a work of nonfiction. This impressive group of nonfiction writers taught me three major lessons about what they do, and each one has strong implications for the classroom.

Lesson One

The first lesson I learned is that nonfiction writers become students of their subjects. They don't take only their *writing* seriously; they take their *learning* seriously as well. When Fred Hechinger reviewed Bill Zinsser's *Writing to Learn*, a book on nonfiction writing, in the *New York Times*, he said, "His book is not just for those who want to be writers, but for anyone who wants to learn anything." At the Teachers College Writing Project we've learned that writing is not mere desk work; rather, it's life work. Whenever our staff members visit New York City teachers to help them turn their classrooms into reading-writing workshops, they see again and again that nonfiction courses of study cannot be confined within four walls. Nonfiction writers do not simply sit at their desks with pen in hand or word-processor at the ready. They're out there, taking in the world, aggressively trying to learn more.

It came as no surprise to me that one Christmas when each of us at the Writing Project was given a chance to select books off a warehouse shelf as a holiday gift, Ralph Fletcher's choices included *The Audobon Guide to Native American Trees* and *Native American Wildflowers*. When my colleague Dorothy Barnhouse and I were teaching an institute in Portland, Oregon, one woman came to class with an invitation from her husband—a pilot: "He's offered to take you on an aerial tour of Mount St. Helen's." It came as no surprise to me that Dorothy went eagerly, while I nervously declined. It came as no surprise to me to learn that when Jean Fritz (1986) was asked about her nonfiction history writing, she reminded her audience that the word "history" comes from the Greek, meaning to inquire into or to ask questions: "I write for my own self because I want to learn. I have a lot of questions," she said. These people, writers all, have a passionate need to know that fuels their work and their lives.

Running alongside this need to know is a willingness to stick with it. When writers find a subject that intrigues them, they are willing to dwell on it, to become totally absorbed, and sometimes even to become obsessed with the desire to learn more and to communicate that learning to others. The young writers in our classrooms need to develop this same hunger for learning and enthusiasm for communicating what they find out.

Lesson Two

The second lesson I learned is that early in their writing process, nonfiction writers want to claim as their own the information they uncover. They want to think new thoughts about it and make new connections that will enhance and expand their learning. They want to come up with a new perspective, a different angle, a personal interpretation. Jane Yolen talks about this in *Writing Books for Children*:

> At first I had an assortment of facts: kites began almost 3000 years ago in China; religious kite flying is done in Japan; intricate centipede and dragon kites abound in Korea; weather kites were important in America; Marconi used a kite antenna for his wireless experiments; Benjamin Franklin flew a kite in a thunderstorm and proved the sky was full of electricity. Lots of data. But then I began to see a common thread, a theme—kites rose in the East and flowered there in beauty and serenity. When they traveled to the West, they became useful. And *that* is information. Once I had that, the book began to achieve a balance, a point of view, a style, and all because I had found a thread that could wind through the narrative of my kite history (1983, p. 70).

Can our students do what Yolen has done? Can they learn to look at information and see in it not a collection of dry facts but something that can be interpreted and then expressed in their own personal way? Margaret Queenan, a colleague from Connecticut, suggests that students can do these things if they have what she calls "that playground tone" when they approach a writing task. "When they look at their data, they need to ask, 'Who says? Wanna make something of it?'" she says. "They should want to make something of it: they should want to take their data and use them to create their own new thoughts and ideas" (1986).

The problem with traditional school reports is that they often contain a restatement (or, at worst, a direct transcription) of the collection of facts students have uncovered about a topic. They express no opinions and convey no sense of their authors' voice or unique interpretation of their research. I've heard them described by Scott Johnson of the *New York Times* as "a regurgitation of someone else's information—mere stenography." The classic report on a topic such as New York state, the sort of thing I had to do in the elementary school I attended as a child, is what Jack Wilde once described as "an essay test without a question"—writing with no authentic audience and no authentic purpose. With the dull, dry listing of facts I would produce, all I did was prove to the teacher that I had looked up the state capital, bird, and flower, the names of rivers, mountain ranges, and cities, and the major products, industries, and leaders.

Several years ago I came across a third grader's report on butterflies. Cassi's report itself was highly reminiscent of encyclopedia writing, but the epilogue was quite different. In that portion of her piece, entitled "What I Think about Butterflies," Cassi wrote, "I feel that it is unkind to keep these wonders of nature in jars. It is unfair to the butterflies because they do not have enough room to live out their 21 days. They do not have enough room to flutter about the flowers or die in a pile of leaves. Fellow girls, boys, and grown-ups. Why capture these marvelous creatures in jars?" Cassi had probably been taught somewhere between kindergarten and grade three that in a report, she was to restate facts, not give opinions. But she had opinions and she wanted to share them, so she tucked them away in the epilogue. And it was only in the epilogue that her voice, her chutzpah, shined through.

Even older students can fall into the trap of giving "just the facts," particularly if they have been asked to write the "classic report" over and over again throughout the grades. Several years ago I heard an English professor at Harvard describe an assignment he gives each year to the first-year undergraduates in his expository writing class: "There's a lovely old building here called Memorial Hall and each year I ask the students, 'What did the builders have in mind about this college, the Civil War, and the United States when they designed Memorial Hall?' Inevitably all the students get up to head for the library, but I tell them, 'No! There are no answers there. You need to come up with your own. Spend time in Memorial Hall, put the visit together with your own experiences, and think your own new thoughts.'"

In a way it's not surprising that these college students assume that the answers are all in the fact-filled books in the university library, just waiting to be sifted out and regurgitated in an essay. In all likelihood, this assumption has been at the heart of their expository writing since elementary school, and it probably has served them quite well. It is not, however, what professional writers of nonfiction first think of when a new idea suggests itself or is suggested to them. We should work to help children think like *those* writers. Rather than letting our students make a dash for the encyclopedias to find the facts to restate, we should encourage them to wonder, explore, interpret, and develop their own way of thinking about and expressing what they find out. We will end up with students who think more critically and creatively—and their writing will be far more interesting to read.

Lesson Three

The third lesson I learned is that nonfiction writers know their options. They know the world of nonfiction writing and they have an image of where they're headed. They ask themselves, "Who is my audience? What might I do with this information? Is this article suited to one of those airline magazines or would it do better in a technical journal? Or should I try crafting it as a picture book for young children?" Once they've made a tentative decision about form, they begin reading that genre with vigor. Teacher-researchers, for example, study the journals they hope to be published in; they read *Learning, The Reading Teacher,* and *Language Arts* in a new way. They begin to do what Smith (1983) describes as "reading like a writer," and they ask themselves, "How do these teacher-researchers make me so interested in what they have to say? What can I do that they did?"

Dorothy Barnhouse, a writer working with the Teachers College Writing Project, often directs the members of her adult writing group to "find a short story you're jealous of, one you wish you had written." This serves as the inspiration or the guide for their own writing. When we make similar suggestions to students who are embarking on nonfiction writing, we should hope that they'll choose well-written books over encyclopedia and textbook passages. We should make sure that our students know what Madeleine L'Engle knows: "We go to encyclopedia for facts but stories and poetry for truth." We should make sure they take to heart what Kathryn Lasky says: "Facts are cheap. Real stories are rare and expensive" (1985). And we should ensure that there are numerous examples of high-quality exposition available in our classrooms.

Classroom Implications: Collecting Data

What do these three lessons mean in terms of how we live our lives in the classroom? In my dream classroom, each student would have a filing cabinet, a desk with drawers, and access to telephones and telephone directories, stamps and stationery, appointment books and calendars, cameras, tape recorders, photocopiers, books, and file folders with tabs to categorize their data. These are all things you or I would need to conduct careful research; these are all things we'd need to be powerful learners, to be students of our subjects. The real world is full of constraints that make this ideal impossible, but most of us can at least provide the young writers in our classrooms with file folders or envelopes or shirt boxes—anything they can label and decorate to serve as special storehouses to fill with research data on a topic.

Then, of course, we need to share with our young researchers many strategies for collecting information. The first thing they need to do is find out what they already know. "Collecting," says Peter Elbow, "begins with *re*collecting." How frustrating it is to read a dull report on box turtles copied from an encyclopedia, and then find out the student shares a bedroom with a box turtle.

Our students also need to become "public" learners. They need to let others know that they are looking for information, that there are things they want to know. They need to do what aspiring writers do each Sunday in the *New York Times Book Review*: they need to post authors' queries and make public their requests for information. Recently I've begun to ask students, "What does your mom think about your ideas for a piece on your gerbil?" and "Is your father surprised you're studying the garment center?" The children often respond with surprise; they never thought to talk about their writing or to ask questions about it at home. They continue to consider writing to be school work, something to be thought about only when sitting at a desk in a classroom or reading an encyclopedia entry in the library.

When I'm working on a new topic, I can't help but talk about it. I weave it into every conversation I can because I know that you never know who knows something. Our students need to know that, too.

Another important part of data collection is observation. Consider Roald Dahl's vivid description (in a biographical sketch put together by his publisher) of an event he observed carefully many years earlier: "When I was nine, a man took my adenoids out in Norway with no anaesthetic. Now, fifty-six years later, I can remember every tiny detail including the chip on the right edge of the white kidney-shaped enamel basin the nurse held under my chin to catch the red lumps." Our students need to know how and why to pay careful attention. We need to send them out on research missions with clipboards, reporters' pads, and notebooks.

Not only do writers spend a great deal of time simply observing, but they wonder about the significance of the details they're seeing and jotting down. Journalist Roy Peter Clark says in

Free to Write that "the ordinary person walks down the street and sees a bar, a wig shop, a grocery store, a pharmacy, and a shoe store. The writer sees dozens of story ideas behind the facades of those businesses. He sees people and issues and asks himself, 'Who drinks in that bar at nine in the morning? What kind of market is there for those huge rainbow-colored wigs in that shop window?'" (1987). And so, too, our students must learn how to ask questions and make connections about what they see.

Interviewing is another primary means of collecting valuable data. Our students need to know what my colleague Pat Wilk knows from her days as a journalist: "Interviewing is so crucial that you only know when you're ready to write if you've done enough interviewing that you're starting to hear the same quotes over again." Students need to learn how to follow a line of questioning and probe until they get as much information as possible from an interview subject. Students must also learn that good interviewing involves good listening.

Finally, to collect data for their writing, students must read. Samuel Johnson once wrote, "The greatest part of a writer's time is spent reading in order to write; a person will turn over half a library to make one book." When students do read, our questions shouldn't be "How much did you read?" or "What did you cover?" Instead we need to ask the questions suggested by *Times* columnist Scott Johnson):

- What new ideas has your reading helped you form?
- What changes in your viewpoint has it suggested?
- What deeper problem might it now help you solve?

Our students need to view reading as a way to deepen their thoughts.

I had an unusual reading-for-more-information experience. I was talking to my colleague Joanne Hindley about my chutzpah theory of nonfiction writing. We were in a college bookstore in upstate New York. I began flipping through the pages of Jane Yolen's *Writing Books for Children* and came upon her section on nonfiction writing. There, much to my pleasure (but also to my dismay, since I thought I had found my own new angle) was her advice on interviewing:

> *Chutzpah,* the Yiddish word for gall or guts, is what you need in tracking down another source of background material—individuals who can help you. Since researching in books alone often leaves you with a dry, stolid view of a subject, it helps to find someone with a connection to your subject who can give you a new view. Contacting such a person—or persons—often takes guts, gall, *chutzpah* (1989, p. 72).

"So much for my thinking new thoughts," I remarked to Joanne, who kindly pointed out that Yolen's chutzpah theory wasn't as all-encompassing as mine!

Classroom Implications: Thinking New Thoughts

After data collection is well under way, we need to provide students with strategies that will help them claim the information they have uncovered as their own and to think new thoughts about it. Several of these strategies require the creation of bits of "disposable" writing: we can ask students to do many quick writing activities that will help them begin to take control of their information instead of letting the information control them.

Use learning logs. We can ask students to keep learning logs, for example. These informal journals offer a place to think about thinking. In their logs, students can probe, question, and challenge new information. We can ask them to add to their data or map their information; we can ask them to make guesses, play hunches, and draw diagrams. Here the hope is that by so doing they'll see connections, notice patterns, and begin to think new thoughts. We can also invite them to do playful, casual jottings in their logs, as suggested by Elbow's idea of the "instant version." This approach pushes students to write a draft of a report quickly, at an early stage; the process of creating this "instant" first version of a piece helps young writers find their voices and discover new angles. We can also ask them to try numerous different leads to a piece or simply to expand and play with possible titles for their writing.

Vary the materials. Varying the kind of paper the students use for data collection and writing can serve to invite reflection. We can provide paper with very wide margins that allow for comments and revisions to be made easily. We can suggest double-entry ledgers. We can interrupt note-taking by saying something like "Draw two columns. On the left, write what you're sure of so far; on the right, what you're not sure of so far." All this encourages students to *make* notes, not just *take* them.

Provide time to talk. There are structures we can build that help students talk about the information they have collected and to interact with it in new ways. We can, for example, offer students regular times to put away their notes and confer about their ideas. We can suggest they allow thoughts to snowball as they talk with their teacher, a peer, or a parent.

My son, Michael, once had to do a piece of writing on an American author for one of his college courses. He had chosen Ring Lardner because he wrote so much about baseball—one of Michael's passions. Michael came home for spring break that year, and one morning we sat chatting about Lardner. Michael glanced at the newspaper on the kitchen table—the headlines were about the 1988 presidential primaries—and informed me that he'd read somewhere that Lardner had received one vote at the Democratic National Convention in 1928.

"You're kidding!" I chuckled.

"No," Michael answered, "and I don't think it's that outrageous, either. I might have voted for him myself."

"How come?" I asked

"Well, he had a great sense of humor, he expressed himself really well, his name was a household word because of his newspaper column, and he wrote a lot about all-American topics—like baseball and vacations in Florida!"

Michael realized he had found his organizing vision, a new angle, a way to claim the information he had gathered. He titled his piece "Ring Lardner—He Could Have Been a Contender." Talking through ideas helped Michael, and it can help our students.

Set up peer teaching times. What I call "teaching appointments" are another means of inviting students to interact with their information. Students sign up to teach their classmates what they've learned about a topic, with the clear understanding that the learning is still "in process." By sharing knowledge early in the process rather than waiting for publication or presentation of a final piece, students have the opportunity to push and clarify their ideas. They teach in order to hone their thinking and listen for a natural voice in which to present it, a voice worth aiming for on paper.

Surround students with writing. Here I must emphasize again that we need to surround our students with fine nonfiction writing in all its modes. That includes essays and editorials, picture books and poems, interviews and book reviews, speeches and journal articles. Not only are these materials important for data collecting, but they give young writers an image of where they're headed and examples of voices real writers use. Smith (1983) reminds us that "teachers must make sure children have access to reading materials that are relevant to the kinds of writers they are interested in becoming," that we must recruit the authors who become "unwitting collaborators" for our students. But the question is, whom should we recruit?

In adult nonfiction writing workshops our unwitting collaborators may include Joan Didion, Susan Sontag, Stephen Jay Gould, Lewis Thomas, Annie Dillard, William Zinsser, E.B. White, Donald Murray, and even John F. Kennedy, who spoke and wrote with such elegance, wit, and power.

We can spot the great nonfiction writing around us if we read with our antennae out. We can search in newspapers, magazines, and through the books that line our library shelves. We can find many excerpts to put in our own reference files, and we need to invite students to do the same. Who should be our students' unwitting collaborators? Kathryn Lasky, Jean Craighead George, Seymour Simon, Cynthia Rylant, Milton Meltzer, Jean Fritz, and Jim Arnosky come to mind; there are, of course, many others. Children can also read and appreciate the work of their peers. Elizabeth's "panda project" provides a delightful example of children's writing that has chutzpah from start to finish and contains surprising descriptions and clever metaphors:

What They Look Like

Giant Panda

The giant panda looks like a blown up black and white balloon that is just lying down in a pile of weeds. It looks like it doesn't weigh much but it ways 1,000 lbs. Now isn't that amazing!

Red Panda

The red panda looks like a deflated basketball with white spots on the bottom. Well, before I started researching I thought the red panda only weighed 8 pounds but...it doesn't. It weighs 80 or 90 lbs.

What They Eat

Besides eating bamboo the panda loves honey. They stick their paws in a bee hive or a honey tree and scoop out the honey for themselves. They like the honeycomb more. When they eat the honeycomb, bees sometimes get swallowed. Pandas, especially the giant panda like cranberries or crabapples. The panda can't find these daily, like you find your breakfast. They have to walk a mile or so to find them.

How They Eat

As I told you about before, pandas like to eat honey. When they swallow bees it won't hurt, because they have a tough padding on their so that a few bee stings won't hurt much.

Pandas are something like raccoons. They wash the food and then feast.

Topic choice. Finally we reach the really big issue: topic choice. Many of us probably feel dread when we recall being asked to write reports for school on topics that were extremely hard to fall in love with, things we were not at all interested in. One teacher described to me a memory she had of having to do a report on the Bessemer process of converting iron to steel. She could hardly understand the books she found on the topic, and her whole family ended up trying to help her. She remembered her father bringing home stacks of tracing paper, her brother painstakingly copying the diagrams from the family's encyclopedia, and her mother staying up late to type the report. But her most vivid memory was of her humiliation at having to stand before the entire class and read a report that she didn't understand. At the conclusion of her presentation the teacher questioned her on the topic. Her lack of understanding was immediately apparent to the other children, who all joined in in laughing at her. "The problem in schools," Don Graves once said, "is that we're always scratching learners where they don't itch." The Bessemer process certainly didn't make this teacher itch.

Many who study the process approach to writing believe that the best way to teach nonfiction writing to our students is to insist that they all choose their own topics. This, of course, ensures that students will be interested in what they're writing about, and we hope that this interest will translate into better writing. This is an ideal situation. There are times, however, when the strength of 35 children choosing their own topics can be seen as a weakness. When so many children each pick a different area of study, who provides a safety net for the research? Who makes sure there are people to be interviewed, places to visit, readable books to be read, first-hand observations to be done? Perhaps those children who choose topics for which there is no available "support system" are the ones who end up copying from an encyclopedia, the only source of information that is readily available to them.

A very different picture emerges in classrooms where everyone works under a large umbrella topic to contribute to a whole-class project that occupies a significant stretch of time. A true community of learners has grown in District 10 in the Bronx, New York, for example, where children each year participate in something called the "City Critter Project." Each child chooses an animal that lives in the city to study and write about. Another community of learners has grown in District 15 in Brooklyn, where seventh graders study how science manifests itself in neighborhood stores. Some become fascinated with the beauty parlor; others study the hardware store or the ice cream parlor. Yet another community of learners has grown on the Zuni reservation in New Mexico, where each high school student has to research a natural resource found on the reservation that is particularly important or significant to him or her. Some choose the herbs their grandmothers turn into shampoo; others choose water because they are so taken with the ceremonies of the raindancers. And another community of learners has grown at a Jewish day school in Miami where in one project everyone writes about Israel, but each child has to think through what really matters to him or her within this very broad topic.

We need to be aware of things that interest our students and to be open to new possibilities for writing topics. The Bessemer process will probably not cause an itch, but I wonder if things would be different if an observant teacher noticed students' fascination with, say, a new word-processor or video recorder. And maybe that teacher would encourage students to talk about the inventions and technological advances that have made a difference in their lives, and ask each student to select one to study carefully. I wonder if each student in that classroom would become part of a community of learners filled with experts and enthusiasm, inventions and readable materials, people to talk to and places to visit. And if all this happened, would those students' writing then be filled with energy and chutzpah? I think there's a good chance that it would be.

This is not to suggest that we revert to assigning writing topics, but rather that we consider providing occasionally a carefully selected "umbrella," a broad subject that allows for many individual topic selections, particulary for the beginning nonfiction writer, in overcrowded classrooms, or in settings in which children have no access to exploring on their own outside of school. There is much to be said for whole-class projects: they lead to a real sense of community; they punctuate the school year by giving a dramatically different feel to the writing workshop; they prompt detailed exploration of topics as children go off in different directions; they show students what it's like to dwell on, probe, and stick with a topic; and most of all they provide students with a safety net against failure.

Chutzpah and the Writing Teacher

I want to end by talking about teachers, because not only does it take chutzpah to write nonfiction well, but also to teach nonfiction writing well. It takes guts and gall to carve out big blocks of time, to stop worrying about covering the curriculum, and instead to follow the advice I have heard David Hawkins give to *uncover* the curriculum. It takes aggressiveness and brazenness to ask for a little bit of money for books and stamps and trips and duplicating.

Most of all it takes chutzpah to give ourselves what we work so hard to give our students: we worry so much over our students' learning that we often neglect to take care of our own. We are students, too, and we need time to read, to take notes, to do first-hand observation, to interview, and to confer with colleagues. When visitors come to our schools we should hope they will say, "What a community of learners has grown here." But they should be talking about our staffrooms as well as our classrooms.

References

Calkins, L.M. (1989). *The art of teaching writing*. Portsmouth, NH: Heinemann.

Clark, R.P. (1987). *Free to write: A journalist teaches young writers*. Portsmouth, NH: Heinemann.

Fritz, J. (1986, July/August). There once was. *Hornbook, 62*(4), 432-435.

Lasky, K. (1985, September/October). Reflections on nonfiction. *Hornbook, 61*(5), 527-532.

Ohanian, S. (1987, May 6). Finding a 'loony list' while searcing for literacy. *Education Week*, 21-22.

Queenan, M. (1986, November). Finding the grain in the marble. *Language Arts, 63*(7), 666-673.

Smith, F. (1983, May). Reading like a writer. *Language Arts, 60*(5), 558-567.

Yolen, J. (1983). *Writing books for children*. Boston, MA: Writer.

Chapter 3

Modeling the Process Approach in the Early Elementary Grades

Virginia C. Schroder
Ann K. Lovett

Writing used to be the first thing to go if, when we were planning our lessons, it looked like we might be short of time for teaching other topics. It is a tricky subject, not easy to commit to syllabus, except in terms of mechanical skills such as spelling, punctuation, and tenses. Somehow we were always aware that writing was far more than this, but we couldn't put our fingers on how to define or teach about those missing elements so they would be meaningful to young children.

We knew that we had problems in teaching writing and needed help, so we asked to attend a conference on writing being conducted by Nancie Atwell. We taught as a team and felt strongly that we should learn as a team, so we were delighted when we both received approval to go. But even on our way to the conference site, our negative attitudes about teaching writing surfaced:

> Ann: What did you leave for your substitute to do today?
>
> Ginnie: No writing, that's for sure! The kids aren't crazy about it, and if it's hard for me to teach it, I figure it'd be even harder for a sub. I'll stick in a writing period later this week—maybe.
>
> Ann: You mean, unless it rains or there's a special assembly or the kids need a longer recess....

We laughed together, but we realized we had a lot to learn.

As we listened to Nancie Atwell that day, we took notes furiously and we talked all the way home about what we had learned. This was the beginning of our development as writing teachers. We became committed to taking a risk and changing the way we approached writing in our classrooms.

Atwell's workshop, and her book *Making Every Student a More Skillful Writer* (1984) that we obtained there, introduced us to the idea of thinking about and teaching writing as a process. By modeling how writing is done rather than simply evaluating a finished piece, teachers find that students enjoy writing and learn more from it; gradually children begin to write with greater interest and stronger voices and, with practice, to become more adept at writing mechanics (see, for example, Atwell, 1987; Calkins, 1986; Graves, 1983). The writing process is generally seen to consist of five main steps: *prewriting,* which involves brainstorming for ideas and refining writing topics and approaches, often by means of group discussions; *drafting,* or the preparation of an initial written text; *revising,* in which aspects such as clarity and style are worked on, often after discussions with peers or the teacher; *editing,* the stage at which a draft is checked for spelling, punctuation, or grammatical errors; and *publishing,* or the sharing of written work with others in some way.

In the past, we had provided students with a limited choice of writing topics; now we decided to let them find their own ideas, providing guidance as necessary. Although we were concerned that Atwell's ideas, implemented in her own middle school classroom, might not work for our third graders, we were eager to see what would happen.

Evolution

We did indeed see improvement when we instituted what we could of Atwell's ideas with our students. We found that the children took more ownership of their writing—and, therefore, more care with it—if they chose their topics themselves. Although many pieces were still of the bed-to-bed variety, some had a stronger sense of the author's voice; they no longer seemed artificial or manufactured.

Management continued to be a problem, however. In trying to meet the needs of children struggling to begin their drafts, those stuck somewhere in the middle, and those needing to come to an ending, we discovered we were still missing the words we needed to help them with their fine-tuning. How could we get these young writers to look back on what they'd written and get a sense of what was missing in their pieces? We felt that if we gave them too much advice, their stories would become our stories, and we'd be back to the cookie-cutter pieces we'd always had. We had many discussions about these issues, along these lines:

> Ginnie: The children are so enthusiastic about writing now. They can't wait to start our quiet writing time each day. I think some of their topics are still too broad, but they are really taking ownership of their writing. I'm really excited about the changes I see.

> Ann: I see the same reaction in my class—the kids like to write now, and they're trying to live that "writer's life" we've heard about. Don't worry about their broad topics; I think that problem will lessen as they share ideas with one another

and as they work more on revision techniques. Don't you see them discussing things among themselves more effectively? They seem more willing to share their efforts and to accept ideas from their peers.

Ginnie: Yes, and this way we're not taking control of their pieces away from them.

Ann: You know, I still need something else. All my students know the steps of the writing process, but very few apply the steps by themselves. How can I help them?

Ginnie: Hmm, I'm not sure. I think we should do some more reading. We've now become familiar with the names of some excellent authors on the subject. And perhaps Judy [the library media specialist] can advise us.

Ann: Great idea! We can also contact the district's Teachers' Resource Center and ask Irene [the principal] for a list of writing conferences....

And so we sought advice from periodicals, attended Saturday workshops at Columbia University Teachers College, and read books such as Lucy Calkins's *The Art of Teaching Writing*. We found a piece that seemed to be missing from the puzzle when we attended another writing workshop, this one conducted by Shelley Harwayne, one of the authors in this volume. She demonstrated how to model each phase of the writing process for children and showed us ways to keep the control where it belongs—in the hands of the authors—while helping students see what they can do to improve their work and make it more interesting. We realized that this was a way to draw our youngsters from a private writing world, where a basic idea or two evoked the whole fabric of a special event for them but left other readers floundering without any sense of moment. Modeling how to choose what is important in a piece of writing and how to embellish it would also help our more wordy writers cut through the unnecessary stuffing that often threatened to smother their pieces.

There was another, perhaps more subtle aspect to Shelley's presentation which we incorporated into our emerging philosophy of teaching writing: she showed us how important it was to give students frequent opportunities to write and how vital it was that they saw us as writers, too. We now try to share our writing with students and to write in front of them whenever possible. We know that when we share the development of our own stories, the whole class becomes a community of authors. We are all in it together; we learn from one another; we share ideas that work, we discuss why some things work better than others, and we explore the myriad choices open to authors along the paths of their writing. While maintaining an atmosphere of quiet purpose, we now confer with our students as colleagues whose expertise and advice we respect and not just as beginning writers who need our help.

The following sections provide an example of the steps we now take when we have writing times in our classrooms.

Step 1: Prewriting

This step involves topic choice and gives us an immediate opportunity to model our own writing processes. If we want children to write freely, they need to understand that their choice of topic is in no way limited by their control of the conventions and mechanics of writing; they also need the stimulation of sharing potential topics with one another, trying out selections and accepting, revising, or discarding them as need be. Children sometimes stick to the same topic because it has few risks for them—the words are the same, the language flows easily, the feelings don't surprise. Sometimes they need to be guided to new choices and experiments that will broaden their writing experiences.

In the early days of the school year, we often get things going by asking students to think of some stories they would enjoy writing. Slowly, then more confidently, the children volunteer their topics, which we list on the board. Typically their topics are too broad. Later we'll have a lesson on focusing or narrowing topics but, for now, all ideas are accepted.

We try not to stop the flow of the children's ideas, but as they begin to dwindle we move on eagerly to the next phase of the process. Class discussions at this stage usually sound something like this:

Teacher: Fluffy the cat, school, trees, baseball, Judy's vacation...this list looks wonderful. If I had to pick one of these topics to start my writing tomorrow, I'd have a tough time choosing just one. But, let's see.... I also went on a vacation. Judy, that was your suggestion. Where did you go on your vacation?

Judy: I went to my grandma's house. She lives in Pittsburgh.

Teacher: Oh, too bad! I've never been to your grandmother's. I don't know her or anything about Pittsburgh. *You* certainly could write a good story about your vacation, but I would have a lot of trouble.... But I know—I went on a vacation to Japan! I know a lot about Japan now. I bet I could write a good story about *my* vacation.

Okay—but maybe there's something I'd rather choose from our list. Matthew, you said you'd like to write about Fluffy the cat. You know all about her, don't you?

Matthew: Yes, 'cause I've had her since she was just a kitten.

Teacher: Then you certainly could write a lot about her. But I've never met Fluffy—I don't know what she looks like, what cute things she does, or anything else about her. I couldn't do a good job with this topic.... Hey, I know! I have a wonderful dog named Skipper. I know all about him!

We continue to discuss topic choices in this way until the children understand the objective: to choose topics they are interested in, already know a lot about, or want to study.

The children respond to one another's ideas and then make their own lists of possible topics in their journals. Just as with professional authors, children need time to think about their writing. They add to their topic lists at any time. When children find that choices are difficult to make, we help them decide by conferring with them. A title may sound exciting, but it needs detail to support it. We eliminate topics when we can't remember what was special about them.

Step 2: Drafting

Once the children have settled on their topics, they begin to write. We are often delighted to note that the children see themselves as experts on their topics; this, we believe, is due—at least in part—to the fact that they have made their own decisions about their writing choices. We encourage the children's positive views of themselves and remind them to tell all that they know about their topics—not only the factual information, but also their feelings.

We are aware that young writers often "talk between the lines" of their writing—that is, they assume we experienced what they experienced—and leave out large chunks of information in their drafts. To them, their stories are perfectly clear. If someone asks a question, they just fill in the gap off the cuff...and off the paper. We have also noticed that some children can add only to the beginnings or endings of their pieces. They understand that something is missing, but they can't see where best to insert new information.

When we model the drafting stage, we use very rough versions of our pieces, in which we deliberately leave holes. With a little prompting the children will ask questions about the missing information. In this way, we demonstrate how information can be added or deleted from a draft. In this step, we also begin to highlight the "author's voice." We try to show students how to seek out the reasons behind their topic choices, question their motives for writing, and avoid creating stories that cause readers to say, "So what?" Sometimes this process leads students to revise their topic selections. They begin to understand that if they have little invested in their topics, they will have no interest in revising their drafts and their lack of interest will be conveyed to their readers.

Our modeling of the drafting stage usually follows this pattern. After a quiet writing time during which there is no talking or movement about the room, we share our (deliberately bland) stories. We begin by saying something along these lines: "Yesterday we talked about choosing topics. My first topic is Japan because I really enjoyed going there and I now know a lot about Japan. I worked on my story a bit last night, and I'd like to share my first draft with you." We hand out photocopies of the story to the children and display a transparency of it with an overhead projector. The children read the story silently and then we discuss it with them. Generally they are initially confused and reluctant to comment on or criticize their teacher's work, but gradually they become comfortable in voicing their thoughts.

The first draft of the "Japan story" read this way:

> This summer I went to Japan. I saw many schools. I went to many cities. I had fun.

Here is the discussion that followed students' reading of it:

Jodie: It doesn't tell very much.

Eriko: It's very short.

Andre: I don't know what you liked about Japan.

Teacher: Would you like me to add to my story? Please help me decide how.

Eriko: Tell when you went to Japan.

Peter: What did you see in the schools?

Joelle: Which cities did you visit?

As the children ask their questions and make their comments, we record them on the transparency; the children transcribe these on the photocopies so they can use them later to remind themselves of the sorts of things they should remember when drafting and revising. The figure on the next page shows the comments and questions marked on the Japan story.

After thanking the children for their input, we promise to share our subsequent drafts during later writing sessions. The children then have the opportunity to continue working on their initial drafts, rereading and thinking about questions other readers might have if they read the pieces.

Step 3: Revising

Children, especially very young ones, have a fierce pride in their writing. They are delighted at their developing skills and often regard every word they write as a jewel. Their young egos immediately approve of whatever they write, and it is often difficult for them to shift their perspectives to become readers and critics of their own work.

It takes a great deal of patience and an atmosphere of trust to persuade young authors to revise what they have written. One way we encourage revision is to allow children to confer with peers *as* they are drafting their pieces, rather than waiting until after the first draft is finished. This way they can think about revising before the piece becomes too long, thereby making the task less onerous. We also have to remember, though, that at the third grade level (and certainly in earlier grades) there is a difference in physical maturation among students. For some, the lack of fine motor control actually makes writing physically exhausting; with these children revision comes in small steps.

Our more able authors sometimes fight revision for a different reason: they see it as a tool for the less capable. These authors pride themselves on their "perfect" first drafts. We have to convince them that revision does not mean admitting weakness or failure. Sometimes simply asking these youngsters what they plan to do next—keeping the options open and the reins in their hands—is enough to prompt the beginnings of a change in attitude. We also make sure these students, along with their classmates, are aware of

Revising the Japan Story

Draft 1

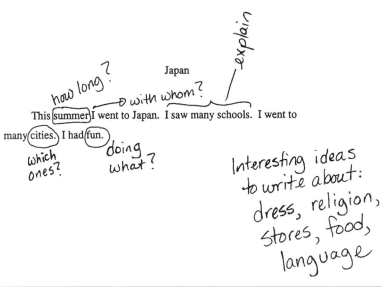

our own willingness to revise, and we often praise students openly when we see the giant steps being taken between drafts.

At this stage in the writing process, a lesson might follow this pattern. After a quiet writing time during which the children are encouraged to work on revising their first drafts, we hand out a second draft of our own stories and display a copy on the overhead projector. The children read silently and then are asked to react to the revisions that have been made to the first draft.

Our second drafts are purposely unpolished and still lack considerable information and detail. At this stage, for example, the Japan story went this way:

> This past summer I went to Japan for to weeks. My husband and I were with a group of twenty people. We went there to visit and study the Japanese schools. We learned that Japanese

children go to school for half a day on saturday and also in July. Usually the class does the same lesson all together at the same time. I saw many interesting cities such as Tokyo, Kyoto, and yokahama. It was fun to eat Japanese food with chopsticks. There language is very different but I learned some words. there are two main religions in Japan—shintoism and Buddhism.

When the students read this, they responded eagerly, asking what was interesting in the cities, what kinds of foods the Japanese eat, what the Japanese wear, and for some examples of Japanese words.

Comments and questions are noted on the transparency in the same way as at the drafting stage. Occasionally the children will suggest including something that we would not choose to write about, and this provides a good opportunity to discuss the concept of ownership. Children are often thrilled to learn that, as authors, they are the ones who decide on the content of their pieces. We then provide time for the children to begin revising their drafts.

This process of revision may be repeated many times. It usually takes numerous conferences and writing periods before children feel that the content of their pieces is set. Certainly all will not be at the same level in their writing, despite careful modeling of the process. For some, voice will remain an issue; there will be pieces that seem to have little personal involvement and there will be children who steadfastly resist undertaking the effort to revise. Still, we have found that by following this procedure our students have come farther than ever before in terms of selecting and narrowing their topics, so they can at least finish a piece before it overwhelms them. This is certainly a significant step.

Step 4: Editing

From the beginning, we deliberately misspell words, omit proper punctuation, and make grammatical errors on the drafts we share with the children. These are often the first things the children point out when we ask for suggestions for improving our drafts— they are horrified at the number of easily recognized mistakes their teachers have made! When this happens, we remind students that in the drafting stage the mechanics of writing are not as important as concentrating on getting thoughts and information on paper; mechanics can wait till later. "Later" comes at the editing stage of the writing process. At this point we ask students to find the errors in our drafts and we model the use of proofreader's marks on our pieces. To help children with the editing step, we hang display charts and lists around the room so accurate examples are always visible (a "When to Use Capitals" wall chart, for example), provide time for peer or teacher-student conferences, conduct minilessons on mechanics, and encourage the children to confer with one another to edit their own drafts.

Just as with the other stages of the writing process, editing is an individual step. Some children are ready to grasp the intricacies of paragraphing and quotation marks; others still need help with ending punctuation. We work as a community to ready pieces for publication, and we celebrate the drafts as much as we celebrate the polished, finished pieces.

Step 5: Publishing

Depending on the purpose of the writing, publishing takes many forms. Some pieces are shared within the classroom and then filed into portfolios. Others are "bound" between simple covers and displayed in a classroom collection or in the hallway. Whatever the form or format, final copies are celebrated. We recognize the effort they represent, from first drafts to finished pieces.

Publishing requires that written work be brought to a certain level of accuracy. The audience needs to be able to read what has been produced, and we, as readers, have learned what that means—in terms of both content and mechanics. At the third grade level we encourage children to edit for capital letters, forms of punctuation, spelling (within reason), and paragraphing, but we recognize that not all children will be able to find their errors. So we help one another. In the end, we accept the best of what each child has to offer. Every story is a success!

Learning and Growing

We cannot expect all children to grow equally in writing proficiency; what we can do is offer direction through modeling and frequent opportunities for success. We have seen dramatic changes in our students as the result of our new approach; we now have classes in which children enjoy writing and know the camaraderie of working together, showing one another how to be writers.

Although we have come a long way, we still have much to learn. Lately our conversations have sounded like this:

> Ann: Look at the stories we've published! I'm so pleased with the improvement and the effort I've seen.
>
> Ginnie: Yes, I can see real progress. Most of the children can stick to their topics and develop them with interesting language and details. I think our modeling is working.
>
> Ann: Don't forget—we're going to meet with two other teachers tomorrow to share our strategies with them. I'm so glad they're interested in working with us; both of them have wonderful ideas about writing. They've also done a lot of research on the process approach.
>
> Ginnie: Maybe one of them can give us some tips about management. Even though the children are following the steps of the writing process more independently, I never seem to have enough time to hold conferences with all those I need to see.

Our interest in improving our teaching of writing continues. We have learned and grown along with our students, but at each new phase of our development, there are gaps to fill and risks to take. We need the same safe environment for learning that the children require: support from our peers and the administration, access to sources of information, and the freedom to take chances. As we talk with our colleagues, listen to workshop speakers, and try out new ideas in the classroom, we constantly rekindle our enthusiasm, refine our skills, and explore new ways to strengthen our community of authors.

References

Atwell, N. (1984). *Making every student a more skillful writer.* Belmont, CA: Learning Institute.

Atwell, N. (1987). *In the middle: Writing, reading, and learning with adolescents.* Portsmouth, NH: Heinemann.

Calkins, L.M. (1986). *The art of teaching writing.* Portsmouth, NH: Heinemann.

Graves, D.H. (1983). *Writing: Teachers and children at work.* Portsmouth, NH: Heinemann.

Chapter 4

Organic Mechanics: Developing Skills through Literature and Student Writing

JoAnne Sangirardi-Gray
Elisabeth Meltzer

N ot long ago, we came across an old trunk full of Elisabeth's primary school books, stored carefully in her mother's attic. Rifling through the trove of black-and-white copybooks, gold-starred spelling tests, and mimeographed dittos scarred with red ink, we came eye to eye with some old familiar faces—Dick, Jane, and Spot. Cringing, we both remembered the tedium of our primers, grammar texts, and workbook drills. It's lucky that at home, after we had completed our daily homework drills, we immersed ourselves in favorite books and our own explorations of writing.

As we dug down deeper into Elisabeth's trunk, we uncovered the real treasures of her childhood literacy learning: her cherished children's books. We began to reminisce about the intellectual pursuits that were truly important to us in those days. As children we both made up and illustrated stories, read aloud to younger siblings, wrote and performed plays for our families, and experimented with original poems, riddles, songs, and jokes. We learned to love language as a result of these literacy adventures, almost in spite of our formal language arts education. We try to bring this love of language to our students by creating a classroom atmosphere in which they can explore reading and writing in school in the ways we could only do at home.

During our teacher training, we were exposed to whole language theories and the idea that writing should be viewed as a process. These notions validated our beliefs that children would benefit from an "on the job" or "learning by doing" approach, especially in the area of writing. We eagerly embraced this philosophy of teaching and have tried to put it into action in our fourth and fifth grade classrooms. We are fortunate to teach in the North Shore school district on New York's suburban Long Island. The district is headed by a visionary administration and our school, Sea Cliff Elementary, is guided by an innovative and supportive principal. These factors, along with an involved school community and a class size of fewer than twenty students, enable us to break with traditional teaching modes and to be forward-thinking.

Although we are firm believers in the benefits of this approach to literacy instruction, not everyone is convinced. We receive considerable support from our school administration, but we are often challenged by colleagues and are called on to defend our practices and beliefs. At first glance, our nontraditional classroom environments and approaches can make some parents uneasy.

Parents provide the much-needed support that allows our program and their children to be successful. Because of this, we feel it is essential to clear up any misunderstandings and fears parents may have. One year during the first week of school, the president of the local parent-teacher association appeared at Elisabeth's classroom door looking very concerned. "I hear you are not using books this year," she remarked. She went on to say that her daughter was delighted with her new teacher because she didn't require her students to use books. Needless to say, this was a perfect opportunity to clear up a misperception. Elisabeth explained to the concerned mother that on the previous day she had informed her students that instead of textbooks or workbooks they would be using "storybooks" and "fact books" as learning tools.

In fact, our supposed "avoidance" of books has caused some misperceptions among our colleagues as well. Their criticisms often center on the belief that we do not cover the mechanics and skills of writing, a belief that springs from the fact that we do not use grammar or spelling textbooks. The reality is that we do indeed address the important conventions of written language, but we teach them in unique and exciting ways using literature and our students' own writing. Through our approach, the children in our classrooms become active participants in their learning about writing. They learn and use the steps in the writing process, become good critics of their own and others' writing, and write with greater fluency.

We gain much fulfillment from our efforts and forget the criticisms when we watch our students flourish and become "turned on" to writing and to school. Each morning they arrive excited and open to what lies ahead in the day's activities. On parents' night, our students' attitudes toward school and learning are often commented on with words such as "My daughter loves to come to school. I can't even get her to stay at home when she is sick!" and "I have never seen my child so happy about coming to school before."

We are convinced that our holistic approach is what makes our teaching so successful. Here are some stories from our classrooms.

Quotation Marks and Parentheses

During an editing conference with Michael, a fourth grader who was working on a personal narrative about his pet cats, JoAnne was thrilled to notice that not only had he made his first attempt at dialogue in his piece, but that all the quotation marks and end punctuation were where they should be. Michael had begun new paragraphs with each new speaker, and the format of his lines varied. Since JoAnne hadn't yet introduced dialogue formally in a minilesson, she wondered how this young writer had learned about it. Dialogue had never before appeared in his writing. "Michael," she said, "I am so pleased to see that you have used dialogue in your cat story. How did you learn to do this so well?"

"From a book," he replied, and he ran back to his seat to find the book.

As JoAnne waited for his return, she wondered what he'd present her with. She knew she had not distributed grammar texts or a skills workbook, but perhaps his parents had equipped him with one. Michael proudly strutted back to JoAnne's desk and showed her the book from which he had learned all about punctuating dialogue. It was Madeleine L'Engle's *A Wrinkle in Time*. Of his own accord, Michael had used a piece of literature as his textbook.

Eileen, another of JoAnne's students, wrote in a story, "And then my sister Cathy came home. (She is older than me and part of a set of twins.) She also wanted to pet our new dog...." JoAnne was intrigued. Eileen had used parentheses effectively— an advanced skill. When asked how she knew how to do this, Eileen said, "It feels right. I'm in the middle of reading *The Phantom Tollbooth* by Norton Juster and he uses those parentheses thingies all the time. I think you have to do it that way when you want the reader to know something right then and there, but it doesn't have that much to do with the story but really should be in there."

It is moments like these that tell us our approach is working. We teach the mechanics of writing in context and on an as-needed or as-used basis, not in discrete lessons dictated by a grammar text or rigid curriculum guide. In writing workshop, we try to explain things that are pertinent to students' writing; often during editing conferences we send student writers back to their seats to find an example of how the professional author of the book they are reading has handled the mechanics or skill they are exploring. There is no better time for students to learn about writing than in the midst of writing, because if they choose, they can immediately experiment with a newly learned skill. Our students view their writing as a process rather than a chore to be critiqued by a teacher with a red pen at the ready, and they make frequent connections between their reading and their writing.

In the next sections we describe how our overall philosophy works in some specific teaching situations.

Some Very Busy Spiders

Picture books used as "teaching books" in the upper elementary grades provide many examples of the correct use of writing mechanics. For example, we love to use Eric Carle's *The Very Busy Spider* in a minilesson to introduce punctuation in dialogue. Carle uses dialogue for the many farm animals' appeals to the spider to come along with them for some entertainment. The spider ignores them and diligently continues spinning her web. Although the book is frequently used with preschoolers and in the earliest grades, we have found that even older children enjoy its predictability and pattern.

After an initial shared reading, we take a look at the mechanical devices Carle uses to let the reader know which words are spoken by the characters in the story. Sometimes a second or third reading—with students playing the various animals and the teacher reading the main narrative—is useful. We ask the students to explain how they know when to begin and stop reading their parts. Students' answers commonly allude to quotation marks, often described as "eyebrows," "flying commas," or "twin commas." Gradually the children are able to point out how quotation marks are used in Carle's story, and all sorts of discussions arise about placing commas and end punctuation inside or outside the "flying commas."

Next we invite students to pretend that Eric Carle has hired them to add a character to his book. They can create any character they wish, as long as they use Carle's pattern for the dialogue. This turns into an exciting, cross-curricular project as students write and illustrate their own pages to add to *The Very Busy Spider*. They are encouraged to be imaginative, and the results are invariably

Figure 1
The Spider and the Snail

"Slurp! Slurp!" slithered the snail. "Want to go get some Lettuce?"

The Spider didn't answer. She was very busy spinning her web

delightful. Figure 1 shows one fourth grader's depiction of the spider's encounter with a snail.

Paragraphing with Comic Strips

At an editing conference in writing workshop, Stacy was sharing her revision of a story about her broken leg. She and Elisabeth discussed the fact that there were no divisions or paragraphs in her piece. Stacy earnestly explained that she didn't understand when to start a new paragraph and was feeling a little unsure about using them. Elisabeth suggested a way in which the child could visualize the breaks and make sense of the sophisticated skill of paragraphing. She asked Stacy to think of scene changes due to shifts in time, location, or action in a movie or comic strip. Elisabeth then suggested that Stacy draw a comic strip version of her story, with each frame showing a different piece of action. Stacy skipped back to her seat and began sketching.

Soon Stacy raced over to Elisabeth with the comic strip that illustrated her piece (shown in Figure 2). After Stacy had

Figure 2
Stacy's Comic Strip

shared it, Elisabeth said, "Now compare your comic strip with your written story. Wherever you have drawn a new box in your comic strip is where a new paragraph should begin in your piece." Stacy now found it easy to take her draft and mark it up with paragraphing symbols in preparation for revising it. After practicing the "cartooning method" a few times, Stacy became the classroom expert on paragraphing. Whenever children were grappling with paragraphs, Elisabeth suggested a conference with Stacy.

Peer Conferences

We both encourage students to work together in conferences quite frequently. Peer conferences are important for two reasons: they build self-confidence and self-reliance in student writers and they help teachers with time management during writing sessions. Many teachers we have spoken with feel comfortable with peer conferences during the early stages of the writing process when students are discussing content, but they express uneasiness when it comes to encouraging such conferences at the final editing stage. "How do you ensure that each kid retains ownership of his or her piece? How do you prevent the student editors from red-inking one another's pieces?" they ask.

Modeling is the key. Student-teacher editing conferences should be held first, so children can become familiar with the process and repeat it later with fellow students. Editing checklists for peer conferences can be provided as guides to the types of nonjudgmental questions and prompts students should ask themselves and one another—"Read your story and see if you have punctuated the end of each sentence," for example. Checklists can be compiled with student input, or teachers can use the many existing published versions as models. (One word of warning, however: "editing" means different things to different people. Some published materials that are labeled "Editing Checklists" extend beyond areas of correctness in grammar, punctuation, and spelling to suggest more substantial revisions of content. Such prompts probably are not appropriate for peer conferences.) To avoid marking a paper with red ink, peer editors can make their comments on separate sheets;

self-adhesive notes on which editors can write comments to position next to specific passages are a second option.

We have found that conferences between two students are most effective; larger groups can seem to "pick on" less capable members. Students can choose their own partners, although it is sometimes necessary for the teacher to pair students strategically according to strengths and abilities. It would serve little purpose to pair two writers fond of run-on sentences; they might be inclined to look at each other's work and pronounce it free of error.

Mad Libs and Lollipops

Students need to do more than identify parts of speech on workbook pages if they are to understand and use language correctly. They need to understand which types of words are appropriate for their writing and to use these words properly. We start the school year by playing a name game sparked by reading Ruth Heller's *Many Luscious Lollipops: A Book about Adjectives*. This book not only informs students about when to use adjectives but also shows how best to use them to add details or make comparisons. After we share the book, students choose an adjective that describes himself or herself and begins with the first letter of his or her first name. Thus "joyful Julianne" and "marvelous Michelle" are given a quick, personal, and easily absorbed lesson about an important part of speech—and a sort of subliminal introduction to alliteration at the same time.

Another fun way we teach the parts of speech is through something called "Mad Libs." These are commercially available fill-in-the-blank books that require children to recognize parts of speech and broaden their vocabularies by coming up with wacky possibilities for the missing words. After a minilesson to review nouns, verbs, adjectives, and adverbs learned by rote in previous grades, we ask groups of students to fill in the blanks in these books. We read the resulting silly pieces aloud and laugh at the often hilarious word choices. It's amazing how children who can't recognize a noun in a workbook exercise know immediately that a person, place, or thing is needed when it is their turn to come up with this part of speech for a Mad Lib.

Figure 3
A Student-Written Mad Lib

How to ride a horse

To ride a horse is really, very _____ Adverb
done. All that you really have to know is
that you're in charge. keep you're _____ Noun
back and straight.
Also after ridding make sure you
_____ the horse. Make sure the horse
verb
knows it did a great job.'
Make sure when you tac it up you
do a verry good job so you don't hurt the
_____. After ridding wash the horse,
an animal
because when they get sweaty and hot it feels

_____ .
ADjctive

After they acquire some familiarity with the Mad Lib format, we ask students to write their own versions to share with the class. In this way, students reinforce their knowledge of the parts of speech, use and label them appropriately, and practice their writing skills to craft an amusing piece. The products are shared with the class; one example is shown in Figure 3. Mad Libs like these help make what was previously a drudgery of grammar become an exciting and amusing way to internalize important information.

"Call the Periods Call the Commas"

When we think about how we were taught to use punctuation, we can vividly recall the scent of the purple ink on the countless dittoed worksheets of periods and semicolons our dedicated teachers painstakingly distributed, collected, and marked. Despite our teachers' good intentions, we never really used punctuation entirely correctly in our writing until we came to understand fully how it affected communication. In some cases, this happened well after elementary school.

We employ a variety of methods to help children understand punctuation and use it properly in their own writing. These methods include conducting minilessons during writing workshop, modeling correct punctuation, and discussing particular students' use of punctuation in editing conferences.

An extremely effective way to stress the need for punctuation is to read a run-on sentence without taking a breath. Children will get the message immediately when you run out of air before reaching the end. When we use this technique we follow it up by asking a student to read Kalli Dakos's poem "Call the Periods Call the Commas" from *If You're Not Here, Please Raise Your Hand*:

> Call the doctors Call the nurses Give me a breath of
> air I've been reading all your stories but the periods
> aren't there Call the policemen Call the traffic guards
> Give me a STOP sign quick Your sentences are running
> when they need a walking stick Call the commas Call
> the question marks Give me a single clue Tell me
> where to breathe with a punctuation mark or two

We then ask the student to punctuate the poem so it can be read without having to "call the doctors."

This activity also provides a good opportunity to stress the idea of audience. Student writers need to keep in mind that their work will eventually be read by someone else and to learn that the conventions of written language are necessary for effective and clear communication.

Organic Spelling

Mechanics and spelling are not sexy. Perhaps this is why there are few practical resources available to help the whole language practitioner who needs to teach some concrete lessons in these areas. At a workshop we conducted at a recent conference, we discovered that many participants were most interested in the topic of our "organic" and individualized spelling program. (We call it organic because students' personal word lists grow from their own writing.) "How do you keep track of all those spelling lists? How do you make sure all the appropriate words are being memorized?" they asked.

We explained that our students begin each week by identifying seven words from their own writing that they know they have misspelled or that we have indicated in an editing conference are misspelled. (We chose seven as the number because, according to folk wisdom, the brain can only commit seven chunks of information to long-term memory at one time.) Adept spellers who do not often misspell words in their own writing are invited to choose challenging words from their reading that they think they will need to know.

Most children can identify misspelled words without our help; they have a sense that certain words "look" or "sound" wrong. At some time or another, however, all children will have trouble finding an error. One way to help them identify misspelled words is to suggest a proofreader's technique: have them read the piece they have written word for word, but backward—that is, from the last word to the first—circling spelling errors as they go along. This trick works because it is often easier to spot a misspelling in a word without context. If, for example, readers expect to see the word "spider" because of the context of the story or sentence in which it appears, they may not notice if it's actually spelled "spidder."

Sometimes it is necessary for the teacher to help point out and correct misspellings. At a recent editing conference on a piece of writing to be shared at an upcoming authors' tea, Andrew proudly showed JoAnne his work, saying, "My story is already edited and now I'm going to write my good copy."

A quick skim through Andrew's piece told JoAnne that there were several spelling errors in it. This posed a problem, since we have a school rule that no student writing may be made public with errors. "Great!" JoAnne said. "But have you corrected all the spelling in your piece?" Andrew nodded his head emphatically.

JoAnne knew that it was critical that Andrew remain in control of his piece and not become dependent on her to correct his errors. She told Andrew that there were still three spelling errors in his story but that he should try to find them himself. Andrew ambled back to his desk. A little while later, he appeared at JoAnne's elbow. "Mrs. Gray, I found two mistakes and I fixed them, but I can't find the other one."

JoAnne now narrowed the field in which Andrew had to continue his word search: she told him on which page of his story to focus his attention. When he still could not find the error, she suggested he focus his attention on a particular paragraph. This enabled him to find the misspelled word. Had he not succeeded, JoAnne would have continued to narrow the field, perhaps winnowing it down from a sentence to two or three words in a phrase.

When all the students have compiled their weekly seven-word lists, they perform the following activities:

- make seven index cards with one word written on each;
- use each word in a sentence on the back of each index card;
- enter the words in personal dictionaries;
- create a puzzle or word search with the words;
- study the words at home and with a partner at school;
- give each other individual spelling quizzes every Friday; and
- spell the words correctly in future writing.

The success of the "weekly words" approach to spelling is clearly demonstrated by students' use of their words in subsequent writing. And that—not scoring 100 percent on a test—is the goal of studying spelling. We consider the Friday quiz just part of the practice; it is students' genuine attempts to use words correctly that we celebrate. Of course, the students sometimes make mistakes, but we view errors as opportunities for exploration of words and language. Not all students are developmentally ready or able to spell correctly all the words they attempt to use. All children, however, can compensate for this by being taught strategies and by being equipped with tools to help them write decipherable pieces. We use dictionaries constantly, have electronic spell-checkers available, and train students to hold peer conferences on spelling.

Probably the most rewarding outcome of our still-evolving approach to spelling is the change in the way children feel about learning spelling. While checking to make sure that the words on her weekly list were spelled correctly, Jessica looked up from her electronic spell-checker and said, "I love spelling! It's my favorite subject now." When pressed for the reason, Jessica replied, "Because these are my own words from my own writing and I like to know how to spell things the right way."

Childhood Treasures

Our students have many opportunities to practice their new and developing skills in the writing they do in our classrooms. We write constantly, whether in plant journals, reading response logs, adaptations of stories, creations of myths, or "math talk" notebooks. Students leave us with portfolios and folders chock-full of the evidence of their learning and growth. Their work includes research projects, invitations to authors' teas, poetry, class-written play scripts, their own sequels to favorite literature, lists of favorite books they have read, personal dictionaries.... We hope that these treasures may someday prompt nostalgic reminiscences when they are found many years from now, preserved in dusty old trunks in our students' attics.

Children's Books

Carle, E. (1989). *The very busy spider*. New York: Philomel.

Dakos, K. (1990). *If you're not here, please raise your hand: Poems about school*. New York: Four Winds.

Heller, R. (1989). *Many luscious lollipops: A book about adjectives*. New York: Putnam.

Juster, N. (1961). *The phantom tollbooth*. New York: Random House.

L'Engle, M. (1962). *A wrinkle in time*. New York: Farrar, Straus & Giroux.

Chapter 5

Writing in Response to Reading: A Process Approach to Literacy Assessment

Roger Farr

In recent years, language arts instruction has been changing in many schools because of new ideas that have evolved about literacy acquisition. Teachers increasingly are basing their instructional decisions on theory that views all forms of language use as dynamic thinking processes constructed on individual experiences, needs, and interests. The language arts—reading, writing, speaking, and listening—are seen as interdependent, and many teachers now strive to integrate all language modes in language-development activities. Indeed, the new thinking about literacy learning has led to significant changes in the classroom: teachers rely to a greater extent on children's literature as instructional text, they give students many opportunities to interact and collaborate in their language use and subsequent language learning, and they guide students to develop abilities to analyze their thinking and skills as they read and write.

Parallel to these developments in theory and instruction have come alternative approaches to language arts assessment. These approaches are a response to often-heard criticism about the standardized tests that are frequently used to measure performance (particularly in reading) and to concerns about the way results of such tests have been used. But, more important, they are also an attempt to match assessment to current theory and practice. Most standardized reading tests consist of text passages followed by multiple-choice questions classified by skills and subskills. In contrast, new types of assessment integrate reading and writing, typically by having students write in response to a text drawn from children's literature, and often include optional activities that involve listening and speaking. The assumption is that if assessment involves the full, interactive process of constructing meaning from text, it will yield a much better indication of how students comprehend what they read and how they use language to communicate their responses. The new approaches encourage individual reactions from students (Strickland, 1990); they also promote interaction and collaboration, even during the assessment process, since these elements are seen as essential to the instruction, learning, and abilities the process seeks to evaluate (Petersen, 1986).

The roles of both teachers and students in the assessment process are changed by this new approach. The emphasis on the ongoing and interactive nature of language development and use has restored trust in teacher judgment. The complex nature of the process is seen to be best evaluated by teachers, who can observe students' use of language on a daily basis over an extended period. Students, of course, have an even better opportunity to evaluate their own progress. Thus, the trends influencing language education today include an effort to make children aware of their own language use—of what they are doing or need to do (Baker & Brown, 1984). New evaluation techniques often include students' self-analyses and their individual reactions to reading and other expressions collected over time.

The Need to Integrate Literacy Assessment

Teachers in many schools where instruction has been influenced by new thinking about language arts teaching and learning are questioning whether the standardized tests they used in the past tell them what they want to know about their students' language development. Typical of such teachers are those in River Forest, Illinois. The River Forest School District is a small suburban school district outside of Chicago. The two elementary schools and one middle school that make up the district serve an above-average socioeconomic community. The parents in the community were very concerned about their children's ability to score well on traditional standardized tests so they could be admitted to the best colleges and universities. Since the children on the whole did score above average on traditional assessments, there was not a strong community desire to move to new assessments. Indeed, it may have been because the students scored above average that the community was not excited about new forms of assessment.

Despite the fact that the community was above average in terms of economics and student-achievement levels, there were a number of students in the schools whose performance was low enough to qualify them for Chapter 1 special assistance. In addition, the community had been going through a period in which concerns about standardized achievement levels were beginning to be raised. Some community members felt the test scores should be higher; others were concerned about whether the standardized tests were valid indicators of students' achievement levels. In brief, community members and educators alike had begun debating tests, achievement levels, and many of the issues regarding assessment that are the focus of attention in school districts throughout the United States and beyond.

At the same time, the staff in the River Forest schools, as in many other school districts, was beginning work to improve the writing program. In fact, important developments have been taking place in language arts instruction in River Forest for over a decade

(Farr et al., 1990). Teachers there have increased the number of classroom activities that call on students to write about what they have read; more and more use is made of students' own writing as text for reading instruction; and students are being encouraged to read for information, enjoyment, or other purposes while recognizing the author's intentions and purpose. Because they are aware of the relationship between language use and thinking ability, the River Forest teachers use reading to prompt various kinds of critical thinking—which, in turn, is expressed through the students' writing and talking.

As they adopted these new instructional techniques, the teachers became increasingly aware that the standardized tests they used did not adequately reflect what was happening in their classrooms. How, they began asking, can multiple-choice questions measure the processes of meaning construction fundamental to reading and writing? How can such tests tell what and how our students are thinking? How can they reveal students' developing abilities in language and their growing understanding of themselves and their worlds? The teachers conceded that they got some useful information from traditional standardized tests, and they understood the desire of administrators, parents, and the public to have a dependable, norm-referenced report of students' progress and of the effectiveness of reading and writing instruction. The standardized tests did, after all, produce information that allowed across-the-country comparison of students' performance.

Like any group of responsible educators, these teachers wanted to be accountable, but they felt that the tests they were using did not really report the language behaviors that were developing around them. They began to search for ways that their ongoing observation of students and the students' own day-to-day work could be incorporated in assessment without sacrificing the accountability that the teachers, the administration, and the community all wanted.

Reading-Writing Connections

The teachers' search took them deep into current literacy research. One area of particular interest was the nature of reading-writing connections. Many teachers now go far beyond using literature as models of organization and writing styles and as sources to promote vocabulary development and sensitivities to language (Graves, 1989; Tierney, 1990). As wonderful and beneficial as those uses of literature can be, we know that asking children to respond to literature can reveal how well they have understood the author's intent and the questions, challenges, and expanded meanings it leads them to. And in order to produce a *written* response to what has been read, students must have grasped the content of the piece of literature and have the skills to express themselves in a comprehensible way.

A written response to literature can be as simple as a statement of criticism or delight or as complex as an evaluation of character or theme. It may be as automatic as explaining events the story calls up from the reader's past experiences or as studied as challenging previously held beliefs due to the meanings and knowledge the story reveals (Newkirk & Atwell, 1986). It can be formal or informal, self-contained or open-ended. Regardless of its form, the summarizing, synthesizing, and selecting of details necessary when writing this sort of response to reading surely reveal comprehension—and thinking and learning—more accurately than do selecting and checking off answers created by a testmaker. In addition, this approach has the benefit of revealing something about students as readers. The written responses to reading that accrue over time can reveal students who unquestioningly, and perhaps naively, accept most texts as well as students whose more critical reading habits promote intelligent skepticism, questions that lead to clarification, and a genuine desire to know more about a topic (Siegel & Carey, 1989).

Writing in response to reading has always provided good teachers with meaningful information for assessment. In the past, however, this writing often consisted of the dreaded book report or research paper. More recently teachers have been relying on readers' logs and personal and dialogue journals in which students ruminate about ideas that are at least in part derived from their reading (Gambrell, 1985). These sorts of writing are less artificial than formal reports; moreover, they are ongoing and can give teachers continuing opportunities to consider how students are developing in the language arts.

The Language Arts Portfolio

Teaching methods that integrate reading and writing often have students develop portfolios of written work that reflect their reactions to literature (Reading/Language in Secondary Schools Subcommittee of the International Reading Association, 1990). These working portfolios include a variety of manuscripts at various stages of development; the pieces result from many different classroom activities and reveal their creators' understanding, new ideas, feelings, beliefs, and concerns. With their teachers, students select materials for their portfolios that will demonstrate their progress as thinkers and language users and their individual approaches to and styles of writing. These selections can be written pieces from reading logs or other responses to literature (such as original efforts that reading has inspired), writing logs, journals, diaries, notes taken in response to reading, original stories or poems, or transcripts of interviews with peers, parents, and others (Valencia, 1990). As students compile these things, they are, in fact, conducting an extensive self-assessment of their progress (Rief, 1990). At the same time, the portfolios are a record of things each student has read and an indication of the kind of use the student has made of particular texts.

In a very real sense, portfolios that contain writing in response to reading offer verifiable indications of students' progress as readers, language users, and thinkers and of the success of language arts instruction. Experience has demonstrated that portfolios are an excellent and concrete way of analyzing student strengths and language-development needs. The prime analysts of the material are the individual students and the teacher, but portfolios also can be used effectively when discussing student progress with administrators and with parents (Flood & Lapp, 1989). This analysis is, of course, relatively subjective—but there is nothing wrong with that. For some teachers, portfolios provide the first entry into truly individualized instruction.

Performance Assessment as Part of the Portfolio

The River Forest teachers recognized the value of language arts portfolios for assessing students' progress, but they realized that such assessment could not be normed. And, they argued, norm-referenced scores are what parents expect. When push came to shove, scores on standardized tests still tended to be viewed as the true measure of students' achievement. Except in the area of evaluating the relationship between student and teacher, the language arts portfolio was seen as lacking in authority.

The teachers felt they needed to demonstrate the relationship between material included in portfolios and reading and writing tests. If portfolios were to gain acceptance and prevail as an assessment tool, their tremendous value and relevance would need to be explained to administrators, parents, and the community. What the teachers felt they needed was an assessment to include in the language arts portfolio that would demonstrate the connection between the portfolio and norm-referenced tests. That meant that portfolios should include some writing that could be assessed in a consistent manner across students, classes, and grades. The teachers hoped this would be a way to link the standardized test results that indicated achievement in certain isolated areas with students' broader growth in language use and thinking skills. Figure 1 shows in diagram form how the teachers saw this integrated type of assessment.

Developing the Performance Assessments

Thus began an extensive project that won the River Forest administration's and community's support. After numerous discussions, meetings, and a summer project, the teachers began to devise various writing tasks that could be assigned periodically and assessed in a standard way. The tasks all called for writing in response to reading and reported on achievement in writing, reading, and thinking for specific purposes. Within a year, River Forest students' language arts portfolios contained numerous examples of these graded written responses to reading. In some classes, these materials made up nearly half of each portfolio.

Figure 1
The Path to Integrated Assessment

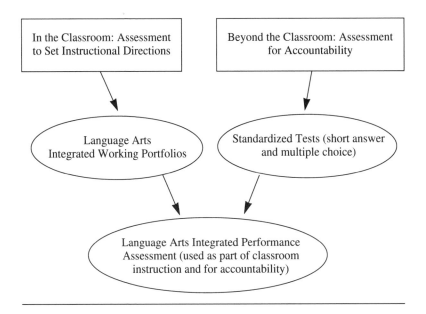

Designing the Tasks

The teachers began by agreeing that all the assessment tasks they designed should reflect their classroom practice. The assignments would therefore approximate class activities, have specific and authentic purposes, and make clear—through examples, if necessary—what was expected of the students. To provide a full range of information for a comprehensive assessment, the tasks would solicit different types of writing intended for a variety of audiences.

Next, the teachers identified types of activities that would reveal comprehension of various texts. These they grouped into three general categories: retelling and synthesizing; extending and predicting; and analyzing, evaluating, and critiquing. The texts themselves were selected primarily from children's literature, according to the following criteria:

- The selection meets a prime requirement of children's literature: it is a good story. It has high interest, good character development, and is long enough to formulate interesting ideas.

- The selection is predictable enough that students are comfortable with it and are eager to confirm what they think will happen. Stories that are not overly complicated and have interesting and familiar settings and characters are best.

- The selection appeals to values and invites unique personal reactions.

- Although stories or descriptions from fiction may make up a majority of the texts selected, some material from articles, interviews, letters, poems, etc., is included. Texts combined with illustrations, diagrams, maps, or charts are used occasionally to promote and evaluate the ability to synthesize information.

Eventually the teachers settled on nine texts for each of grades 1 through 8. These texts they called "prompts," because they would prompt writing that would be evaluated.

Refining the design of the tasks continued after the project was implemented. Groups of teachers began reading and discussing their students' responses in an attempt to identify problems and hone the process. They asked themselves if the prompts and the tasks were well matched. Did they combine to create a relevant experience for the students? Were they getting the sort of writing they anticipated? In order to provide more focus to the assignments, the teachers identified types of writing they felt would reveal the use of certain thinking skills. These were as follows:

- Stories—conclusions to prompts abbreviated by the teacher at a suspenseful high point, elaboration of story events and endings, or an original story based on the prompt.

- Reports—informative writing on a topic, particularly writing that synthesizes information from several sources.
- Persuasive essays—editorial-like solutions to problems or opinions on arguments.
- News or feature articles—such things as newspaper-style accounts of fictional events or explanations of the causes of events in the prompt.
- Letters—to story characters facing particular problems or to the prompt's author.
- Directions or instructions—based on a task described in the prompt.

The teachers hoped that combining appropriate prompts with assignments to create specific types of writing would yield information about students' development of several thinking skills—including predicting, extending, comparing/contrasting, applying/synthesizing, persuading, and evaluating/analyzing. And, of course, the actual written products would reveal students' comprehension of the prompts and their growth in writing ability.

During this development process the teachers also learned that in order to direct the students to the kind of writing and thinking a prompt was intended to elicit—without eliminating room for individual response—the purpose for writing had to be clear and not overly complex. The most effective writing-in-response-to-reading assessment activities were presented with purposes that were brief and to the point, and they reflected real-life experiences and classroom literacy activities. Figure 2 gives some examples of purposes for writing and the activities they could lead to.

Administering the Activity

In addition to refining the nature of the assessment task, the teachers worked to establish the best means of administering it. This proved to be a liberating experience. As the teachers reminded themselves of the need to make assessment worthwhile as instruction and in tune with their classroom reading and writing activities,

Figure 2
Purposes and Ideas for Writing

Purpose for Writing	General Description of Possible Writing Activities
to entertain	• create a new ending or beginning for the story • retell the story in your own words • create a parody of the prompt • create a rhyme, poem, or patter based on the reading
to persuade	• write a letter to one of the story's characters, giving advice or requesting help • write a critical essay about the prompt • write an editorial based on the prompt
to learn	• retell an important event, process, or situation • summarize or synthesize texts • report on a phenomenon mentioned in the text
to inform	• report on a phenomenon mentioned in the text • construct directions or instructions based on something that happens in the text • describe and prepare a critique of the text
to evoke feelings	• describe a personal experience that relates to the text • give an account of what a character might think or feel • create a journal or diary entry for a character • write a letter to a story character or the author of the prompt

all their traditional concerns about how students behave during tests fell away. There was no need to time the test, they found, although they generally made an effort to manage the activity by limiting it to two or three class periods, including time for reading, writing, revising, and editing. The teachers also found that there was no need to worry about whether students assisted one another in responding. Indeed, collaboration could be encouraged—as it was during regular instruction—particularly as part of the revising and editing processes in which input from peers is useful. Each teacher also felt free to advise and instruct students, and the students were allowed to consult references and other sources—just as they would in "real life."

The relaxed atmosphere surrounding the administration of the assessment activity led to increased creativity in the design of the writing tasks. Students wrote letters to advice columns in which they pretended to be story characters in need of help, and they created responses to the letters; they compared works of science fiction with nonfiction accounts of scientific phenomena; they read and responded to movie reviews, historical fiction, and magazine and newspaper articles. The flexibility in administering the activity convinced the River Forest teachers that they were on the right track in the development and implementation of this new means of assessment. Teachers could encourage any student behavior that seemed appropriate, whatever occurred during reading and writing instruction was allowed during assessment, and prompts and tasks could be designed to yield specific information.

Rating Students' Writing

Eventually the River Forest teachers structured and defined a scale, which they called a rubric, for rating students' efforts. One rubric was designed for each specific writing-in-response-to-reading task, but all were patterned on a single model that covered several factors applicable to all types of responses. Using the rubric, teachers could easily, reliably, and with considerable consistency assign ratings to the students' written responses.

The rubric described here and shown graphically in Figure 3 is very similar to the one devised at River Forest. This, however, is a generalizable model intended to serve as the basis for more specific rubrics that can be modified to match the particular goals and instructional emphases of a teacher or group of teachers. This general rubric for assessing writing in response to reading includes factors for reading, writing, and application of the purpose for reading and writing. For each factor, the quality of the response is

Figure 3
General Rubric Design

Rating	Reading	Writing	Application
3	• uses many details accurately • indicates clear grasp of main ideas and important themes	• well organized and clear • vocabulary/usage demonstrate good command of the language	• selects appropriate details to fulfill purpose • uses main ideas/ themes to fulfill purpose
2	• uses some details accurately • indicates adequate grasp of main ideas/ themes	• adequately organized and clear • vocabulary/usage demonstrate some command of the language	• purpose supported with some details • fulfillment of purpose does not contradict main ideas or themes
1	• uses only a few or no details accurately • fails to indicate grasp of main ideas/themes	• poorly organized; unclear • vocabulary/usage indicate little command of the language	• purpose not supported by details • main ideas/themes misrepresented

assigned a number (from 1 to 3 in this case); the numbers are then added to yield an overall score for the reading-writing task. One must keep in mind that the actual criteria for assessment would be far more specific than those described in the figure and would vary depending on the reading prompt, writing activity, and the teachers' particular instructional goals. Some teachers might want to assess how students' writing demonstrates their personal response to and appreciation of the reading prompt, for example; others might wish to expand the rating scale from 3 to 4 or 5, or to experiment with some method of weighting scores in particular areas.

Regardless of the rubric's specifics, however, the subfactors and terminology must be parallel down the columns and across the rows in order to allow for accurate and fair rating. In addition, whatever subfactors are included in each box must be treated as a unit when assigning a rating for that area. This is particularly important when standardization in rating is desired. In this case, numerous raters should use the rubrics in "trial runs" and discuss their ratings of each factor in order to develop a revised rubric that will guide raters with different perspectives to arrive at similar scores for the same piece of writing.

As is the usual case in the development of such rating systems, each rubric devised at River Forest was discussed and revised. The teachers also identified actual student papers that illustrated the individual descriptions in each rubric's grid; these "anchor papers," or clarifying examples, were of considerable help to teachers in rating subsequent student efforts.

Performance Assessment Gains Acceptance

Picking the prompts, designing the writing tasks, determining how they should be administered, writing the rubrics, and selecting the anchor papers is a long and demanding process. In the end, however, the River Forest teachers found that they had begun to structure an assessment that reflected their philosophy of teaching and learning in the language arts.

Although it remains a time- and labor-intensive approach to assessment, the process has gradually become more routine. In fact, the teachers discovered that they could even enlist the help of their students in building a set of writing-in-response-to-reading materials. Occasionally students are called on to discuss the types of writing and thinking they most want to be able to do well, pick stories and other texts that can promote those kinds of writing and thinking (or write their own material to use as prompts), decide on purposes that would direct the kind of writing they want from the prompts, devise rubrics, or create anchor papers to illustrate segments of the rubrics.

So explicable and defensible were the teachers' efforts in River Forest that the school administrators, the local press, and the public endorsed the new assessment as the most valuable indicator of how well students were doing in reading and writing and how successful instruction had been. The new assessment became the official measure—comparable to competency testing in other school systems—used in annual testing (Mills, 1989).

The degree to which the procedure is formalized will depend on how explicable teachers would like the ratings to be to other students, parents, administrators, and members of the larger community and on how useful the ratings need to be in tracking students' progress over time. The more formal and structured the rubrics and anchor papers are, the more consistent the individual teacher can be in assessing the progress of individuals from assessment to assessment.

As long as such assessment is a natural part of instruction it should contribute to student language development. It should not, however, ever take on the solemn air that tends to rarefy most testing environments. And no matter how impressive the set of prompts, writing tasks, and rating materials, it would be unfortunate indeed if its use overwhelmed the use of portfolios, reading logs, journals, informal observation, and the like. Teachers should keep in mind that there are a host of instructional activities that can reveal student progress, including a variety of oral presentations and other forms of expression.

Nevertheless, the writing-in-response-to-reading assessment provides a highly reportable and relatively objective means of analyzing student progress and teaching effectiveness without overlooking the insight both teachers and students bring to classroom activities and achievement. The River Forest experience clearly demonstrates that school systems, schools, groups of teachers, and even individual teachers can develop their own means of assessment to match their instructional objectives. The experience of doing so leads both to more "authentic" indications of students' achievement and to valuable clarification of instructional goals and objectives.

References

Baker, L., & Brown, A.L. (1984). Metacognitive skills and reading. In P.D. Pearson (Ed.), *Handbook of reading research*. White Plains, NY: Longman.

Farr, R., Lewis, M., Faszholz, J., Pinsky, E., Towle, S., Lipschutz, J., & Faulds, B.P. (1990). Writing in response to reading. *Educational Leadership, 47*(6), 66-69.

Flood, J., & Lapp, D. (1989). Reporting reading progress: A comparison portfolio for parents. *The Reading Teacher, 42*(7), 508-514.

Gambrell, L.B. (1985). Dialogue journals: Reading-writing interaction. *The Reading Teacher, 38*(6), 512-515.

Graves, D.H. (1989). Research currents: When children respond to fiction. *Language Arts, 66*(7), 776-783.

Mills, R.P. (1989). Portfolios capture rich array of student performance. *School Administrator, 46*(11), 8-11.

Newkirk, T., & Atwell, N. (Eds.). (1986). *Understanding writing: Ways of observing, learning, and teaching, K-8.* Portsmouth, NH: Heinemann.

Petersen, B.T. (Ed.). (1986). *Convergences: Transactions in reading and writing.* Urbana, IL: National Council of Teachers of English.

Reading/Language in Secondary Schools Subcommittee of the International Reading Association (1990). Secondary perspectives: Portfolios illuminate the path for dynamic, interactive readers. *Journal of Reading, 33*(8), 644-647.

Rief, L. (1990). Finding the value in evaluation: Self-assessment in a middle school classroom. *Educational Leadership, 47*(6), 24-29.

Siegel, M., & Carey, R.F. (1989). *Critical thinking: A semiotic perspective.* Bloomington, IN: ERIC/RCS.

Strickland, D.S. (1990). Emergent literacy: How young children learn to read and write. *Educational Leadership, 47*(6), 18-23.

Tierney, R.J. (1990). Redefining reading comprehension. *Educational Leadership, 47*(6), 37-42.

Valencia, S.W. (1990). A portfolio approach to classroom reading assessment: The whys, whats, and hows. *The Reading Teacher, 43*(4), 338-340.

Citation Index

Children's Book Author Index

Children's Book Title Index

Also available from IRA...

Along with writing, the language arts include reading, listening, and speaking. These four elements overlap and blend in the literacy curriculum, and together they run across teaching and learning in the content areas. *Pen in Hand* is just one of a three-part series that has this idea at its heart. Filled with the same sort of practical advice and sound interpretation of current research, the two earlier publications—also edited by distinguished educator Bernice E. Cullinan—complement this volume and are must-haves for any professional library.

• *Fact and Fiction: Literature across the Curriculum* discusses many innovative ways to use children's books in social studies, science, and math classes. This book will show you how literature can serve as a unifying force in your teaching and lead to more enthusiastic learning across disciplines. (IRA publication no. 380-622, US$15.00, US$10.00 for IRA members)

• *Children's Voices: Talk in the Classroom* describes ways to encourage children's development of speaking and listening skills that will benefit their language arts learning. Drama, storytelling, and literature discussion groups are just a few of the topics covered in this collection devoted to an often-neglected aspect of literacy. (IRA publication number 381-622, US$12.00, US$8.00 for IRA members)

To order *Fact and Fiction* and *Children's Voices*, call 1-800-336-READ, ext. 266 (outside Canada and the United States, call 302-731-1600, ext. 266). Visa and MasterCard accepted; postage included on prepaid orders.